THE VOYAGE OF THE
SS JEREMIAH O'BRIEN

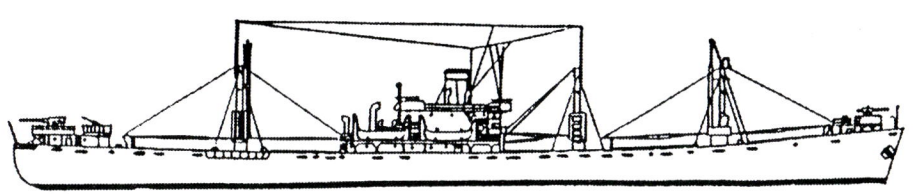

SAN FRANCISCO TO NORMANDY

1994

by
Coleman "Coke" Schneider

10-21-96

To Elsa Cooke Verhylan + Paul

From CEO Glen W. Reed
  Snug Harbor Chapter

and all the members of the

Hampton Roads Chapter

We love you always forever

Never forget you ever.

by Charles Clark Mox Seniorly
   757-247-1656

Coleman Schneider, Publisher
20 Stonybrook Rd.
P.O. Box 625
Tenafly, NJ 07670 USA

ALL RIGHTS RESERVED. Printed in the United States of America by G.T.O. Lithographers, Inc. No part of this publication may be reproduced, stored in a retrieval system, or transmitted in any form by any means, electronic, mechanical, photocopying, recording, or otherwise, without prior written permission of the author.

All precautions have been taken to avoid errors or misrepresentations of facts. However, the publisher does not assume responsibility for, and hereby disclaims any liability to any party for, any errors or omissions.

Library of Congress Catalog Card Number: 94-92400
International Standard Book Number: 0-9601662-5-4
© C. Schneider 1994

Dedicated

to the men and women of the
Merchant Marine, seafarers on
all ships from all countries.

***

They should all sail on ships like the

Lucky Ship,

SS JEREMIAH O'BRIEN

 ## *FOREWORD*

In 1944, those persons on the high seas in Liberty Ships were there for one reason - to help the Allies make the world free. That spirit, which kept the Allies moving towards Normandy and Italy, the Marianas and the Philippines, was backed by millions of supporters on the "home front."

In 1994, those persons on the high seas in Liberty Ships are there for many reasons, but most of all to commemorate the sacrifices made 50 years before. As it was in 1944, such things are only possible because of the strong support from the Allies and the "home front."

I am in the habit of saying, "You are only young once; do it right, and it is enough." When I uttered this comment during the summer of '94, I was corrected by a colleague. "No, those men on that ship are young twice."

Here's to those on the home front, and those at sea, and those Allies who made Liberty Ships welcome in foreign ports. History can be repeated, to some extent. We have just proven it so.

Marci Hooper
San Francisco, California
Business Manager, SS Jeremiah OBrien

INTRODUCTION

This book is the story of an unforgettable ship, the SS Jeremiah O'Brien, and her voyage from San Francisco to D-Day at Normandy, France. She was one of many Liberty Ships that were built in the unbelievable time of 56 days, a feat that may never be accomplished again. But it shows the dedication, workmanship, and planning of American industry in a time of stress. Speed was essential to construct and launch ships faster than they could be sunk. The theme was to build a bridge of ships.

Additionally, the Navy was in similar straits but they had all the experienced labor and shipyards. How could a program of this magnitude of building Liberty Ships be accomplished? How could we possibly hope to build shipyards, train labor with all the skills necessary for shipbuilding, accumulate all the materials and mesh them together to turn out two ships a day?

Well, it happened! A helping hand was given by the Japanese when they bombed Pearl Harbor in 1941; that silenced the anti-war forces and caused them to reverse their positions. That unified the American people and gave them purpose, and they went to work.

733 American cargo ships were sunk by German and Japanese raiders, airplanes, and submarines. More than 6,000 Merchant Mariners were lost during the war, and thousands were injured. Many of those who survived these attacks drifted for days on rafts and lifeboats waiting for rescue. Nearly 600 Merchant Mariners were held as prisoners of war.

This book is also the story of a Kings Point cadet/midshipman in wartime who made the first three voyages on the SS Jeremiah O'Brien in 1943-44, and again made part of the voyages from San Francisco to Normandy in 1994, a chance to relive his nineteenth birthday 50 years later.

Speaking in London in 1944, General Dwight D. Eisenhower said:

"Every man in this Allied command is quick to express his admiration for the loyalty, courage, and fortitude of the officers and men of the Merchant Marine. We count upon their efficiency and their utter devotion to duty as we do our own; they have never failed us yet and in all the struggles yet to come we know that they will never be deterred by any danger, hardship, or privation.

"When final victory is ours, there is no organization that will share its credit more deservedly than the Merchant Marine."

The love of the sea is something intangible that becomes parts of the psyche and never leaves. It is really a comforting feeling that puts the mind and body at ease, but gives you the strength and courage to perform beyond your belief in yourself.

The ship becomes a home, the crew becomes family, working together as brother and sister becomes a natural phenomenon. After 36 years in the reserve fleet, the authors second home, the Jeremiah O'Brien, was restored and reactivated not only as a National Landmark and a museum but as a living, powered mechanism sailing the Atlantic once again, visiting old familiar ports with nary a problem, her machinery sounding like a finely tuned watch, a pulsing heart that never missed a beat.

Additionally, the ship traversed calm seas for a voyage halfway around the world, unlike the days of 30- and 40-foot waves which tested the will of a nineteen-year old cadet.

God was with the ship from the first day a keel plate was laid, and he did not abandon his prize.

ACKNOWLEDGMENTS

The hundreds of thousands of people involved with all phases of Liberty Ships represent almost an entire population: the designers, planners, the people who built the yards, the hundreds of suppliers and their thousands of employees. Their devotion, consecration, and pride are partially responsible for finally winning the war. The final success in freeing Europe from tyranny and saving thousands of lives belongs to the American ethic.

The people directly involved with this voyage of the SS Jeremiah O'Brien are a limited group but still represent hundreds. Many were volunteers who came to work for fun and companionship, or as a hobby, or even to learn. Ten thousand people put in more than 450,000 hours of free time in the past fourteen years, mostly from California. Without them, the voyage would have been impossible.

Foremost among the leaders are Rear Admiral Tom Patterson and the Board of the Jeremiah O'Brien, including Bob Blake, Albert Haskell, Captain Ernie Murdock, Captain Harry Allendorfer, Tom Crowley Sr., Carl Otterberg, and some I've neither heard of nor met.

The Business Manager, Marci Hooper, and her staff held the fort and coordinated all the internal problems about which those on the ship never knew or worried.

The library at Machias, Maine was very helpful.

Carl Nolte's appreciation for the voyage kept his newspaper the San Francisco Chronicle well-informed and in turn kept the public aware of the day-to-day doings of the ship, its position and its activities.

I cannot forget our Reverend James Wade, the only lady of the crew, Mary Steinberg, and of course the rest of the volunteer crew, whose photos and reasons for the voyage are listed in the "Crew" chapter. We are sorry for the crew photos missing; they exist but are not released. All my appreciation goes to the entire crew, who stood the watches and were responsible for the operation, safety, and upkeep of the ship, and also for feeding and caring for us, as well as to those who worked in the Souvenir Shop and helped carry and cover many of the expenses. Also to be commended are the many people and companies behind the scenes who gave of themselves in money, knowledge and assistance; our sincere thanks to all.

Lastly, my thanks to Andersen Silva, who is making his debut as an editor, chosen because of his talent with the English language.

The photos were supplied by Phill Sennett, Ruth Robson, Robert Burnett, the National Liberty Ship Memorial, IWM, NLB, the Lane Victory, Project Liberty Ship, the John W. Brown, the Maine Maritime Academy, the White House, and the Canadian Coast Guard. Photos from World War II on the O'Brien by the Author and Robert Millby, USN, D-Day Museum, and others.

CONTENTS

Foreword	vii
Introduction	ix
Acknowledgments	xi
Contents	xiii

Chapter I
Captain Jeremiah OBrien	1
The Liberty Ships	2
Putting It All Together	5
The Last Convoy 94	10

Chapter II
The Volunteer Crew	12
Deck Department	13
Engineering Department	25
Purser	32
Radio Operator	32
Ships Doctor	33
Stewards Department	34
US Navy Armed Guard	39

Chapter III
Coming Aboard	40
At Sea	47
The Panama Canal	53
The Other Ships	58

Chapter IV
Daily Routine In The Caribbean And North Atlantic	60

Chapter V
Portsmouth	66
D-Day Museum	70

Chapter VI
    In The Solent   76
    The Presidents Visit   77
    D-Day Normandy   82
    Photos, D-Day 1944   86

Chapter VII
    The Cadet   90
    Raising Funds   99

Epilogue   107

Appendix A
    Weather And Position Log, San Francisco to Normandy   113

Appendix B
    Voyages Of The SS Jeremiah OBrien   115
    The Museum Ships   118

Index   121

CHAPTER I

CAPTAIN JEREMIAH O'BRIEN

    Citizens of Machias, Maine were dependent on the sea trade, anxiously awaiting supplies from Boston after the winter of 1775. When the ship arrived, it was accompanied by the British armed schooner, Margaretta, commanded by Captain Moor. The purpose of the escort was to see that the lumber to be brought to Boston in exchange for the supplies was taken back to build barracks for the British soldiers.

    Since news of the Lexington and Concord battles had reached the citizens of Machias, many were opposed to sending the lumber to Boston for the British war effort. To demonstrate their defiance, they erected a "Liberty Pole" made from a tall pine tree, which were to be used only for masts for the King's ships. Captain Moor immediately saw the illegal "Liberty Pole" and demanded its removal.

    After several private town meetings, it was decided the Liberty Pole would remain in the center of town, and they would further the colonies' cause by capturing Captain Moor. The Captain fled on the Margaretta. Soon forty colonists boarded the tiny sloop Unity captained by Jeremiah O'Brien and pursued the Margaretta. Near Round Island in

Machias Bay on June 12, 1775, they engaged the British ship in battle and won. This proved to be the first Naval battle of the Revolutionary War. Captain Moor was wounded and died the following day.

O'Brien captured other British ships later that year as Captain of the privateer Machias Liberty.

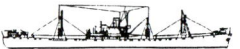 ## THE LIBERTY SHIPS

The Merchant Marine Act of 1936 was passed to reactivate an old, inefficient and run-down American Merchant Marine. The three criteria were:

1. To build a modern and efficient Merchant Marine for national defense and domestic commerce.

2. To design the ships for commerce but make it possible to convert them to naval auxiliaries.

3. To build them in the US, man them with Americans, and sail them under the American flag.

At that time the life of the Merchant ship was estimated to be five years. Fifty ships a year were to be constructed from advanced plans and were to be fast and economical. In 1939, the construction was raised to 200 per year and in 1940 raised again to 400 per year.

In the first nine months of World War II, 150 ships were sunk by German U-boats. This was faster than the English could replace them. The British finally turned to the US to build ships. They brought their own design for a ship that was simple to construct, 10,000 deadweight tons with a 2500-horsepower engine that produced a speed of ten knots and proven reliability.

Gibbs & Cox, a well known company of naval architects, was given the job of modifying the ship design for more simplified construction to meet the needs of the times. The British ordered 60 ships. Modern power units like turbines could not be constructed quickly enough, therefore the engine used was a steam-driven triple expansion reciprocating engine, which was easy to build and operate. President Roosevelt finally approved the modified design, known as a Liberty Ship, in 1941, and, looking at the plans, called it an "Ugly Duckling." The name stuck.

There were no shipyards available for this construction. Most of the available shipyards were busy with orders from the US Navy, and they had the experienced ship builders. New shipyards had to be constructed, labor had to be trained, faster methods of construction were required, and soon the builders turned away from tedious riveting to welding. The first estimate was for 200 emergency class ships. Construction started in

Launching of the Robert E. Peary in 4 days, 15 hrs., 29 mins. (Kaiser Yard, Portland, OR, 11/15/42).

Walter Pidgeon, Adolph Manjou, and Joan Leslie.

Women contributed to manual labor.

1941; by September, fourteen ships were launched around the nation. For 1942-3, another 2300 Liberty Ships were on order.

Construction methods were revolutionized; complete finished parts of ships were built in shops and moved to the ways to be welded in place. Finished superstructures with electrical, toilets, etc., were moved by cranes to set on the deck for welding. Time for construction was to be 110 days; soon we were averaging a new ship every 40 days, and fifteen shipyards were building Liberty ships, employing 300,000 men and women. This was the largest shipbuilding effort ever attempted by man. The US Merchant Marine supplied the largest number of ships, carrying 95% of all military supplies in convoys to all parts of the world.

PUTTING IT ALL TOGETHER

Mass construction of Liberty Ships.

There were 2751 Liberty Ships built from 1941 until the program ended in 1945. They were the backbone of the United States Merchant Marine, used to fill the void in shipping caused by the successful attacks and sinkings by the German submarine fleets.

The Liberties continued in operation after the war ended and were put into service to bring the troops and some war materials back to the US. Many were sold and transferred to foreign governments. As the demand became less hundreds of the Liberties were laid up in eight Maritime Administration National Defense Reserve Fleets.

Foreign crews were used in some cases to bring back the ships to the US when no American crews were available. In England at the Portsmouth Naval Base, I met a seaman who, with fifteen others, made up the crew of many Liberty Ships being returned to the US. These men were smitten with awe when the ships were immediately delivered to a scrap yard to be cut up.

National Defense Reserve Fleet, Suison Bay, CA.

In 1962 the US Navy informed MARAD that they would not require Liberty Ships for future war or emergencies. The ships were not just tied up and anchored, they were carefully maintained in top-notch condition for immediate use should that be necessary. Silverware, linens, galley equipment, charts, ropes, etc., were carefully stowed. Special oil was used extensively to protect metal parts and the ships themselves. The plan was to save the ships for emergency use and quick response. Security at the moorings was intense and few supplies were pilfered.

Gradually, the Maritime Administration (MARAD) sold off various ships for scrap. There are only three National Defense Reserve Fleets left today: one in the James River, on the Virginia Coast; one at Beaumont, Texas; and the last at Suison Bay, California.

Captain Tom Patterson, then Western Regional Director of the Maritime Administration, was directed to survey the ships from the reserve fleet for sales and scrapping. They were to be ranked from best to worst. There were approximately 300 Liberty Ships, at Suison Bay, California; Astoria, Oregon; and Olympia, Washington. He chose the Jeremiah O'Brien as the best ship because it was completely original and had only served for two and a half years in World War II. When lists were submitted for these sales the Jeremiah O'Brien was always the last name on the list.

That was in 1978, and soon a long, difficult endeavor began, involving many people in all phases of the Maritime Industry and the Local, State and Federal Governments. Captain Tom Patterson assembled a group effort and went to work to secure the Jeremiah O'Brien after his superiors in Washington concurred with his plan to make the ship a National Liberty Ship Memorial. A non-profit fund had to be established, monies had to be raised and sponsors found. There was much to be done before they could even consider moving the ship from the Reserve Fleet. Many names enter this part of the transactions, led by Captain Patterson, Captain Harry Allendorfer USNR, Tom Crowley, Bob Blake, Port Captain of Marine Inspection Ernest Murdock, the US Coast Guard, and others too numerous to mention.

The ship was owned by the United States Maritime Administration, chartered to the National Park Service, and operated by volunteers. A group of four shipyard managers were taken for an inspection of the O'Brien. Gayne Marriner, General Manager of the Bethlehem yard in San Francisco, said he would take the ship. She received a first class job, requiring the ship to be dry docked, the whole vessel striped and coated with zinc, repainted, and repaired. Numerous other jobs were performed so she would look and act like a new ship. Bethlehem did a beautiful job!

Money was a factor. A lot had to be raised, since this kind of rehabilitation was very, very expensive. Volunteer labor was sought from people who had an interest in ships, who were willing to give time to fix, paint, and use their skills free. It seemed they were waiting in the wings, for many came to the salvation of the O'Brien. Permission was asked of the Bethlehem yard to allow volunteers to work on the ship, and they agreed, thus cutting expenses by a large degree.

It was determined, while she was still in the reserve fleet, that the ship should be made to steam on her own, rather than towing her to the dockyard. Work began to prepare her, and the ship was ready to go to the yard on October 6, 1979. By this time steam was up and the engine room equipment had been cleaned, checked and tested. Chief Engineer Harry

Morgan was ready, 550 life jackets off the SS Monterey were aboard, and Tom Crowley offered two tugs as well as an excursion boat. Captain George Jahn acted as pilot.

After 33 years in the reserve fleet, the SS Jeremiah O'Brien was released, and under her own power sailed to the Bethlehem shipyard. The fuel used for this trip and the next two years was that in her tanks from World War II.

Assistance was readily available from volunteers, shipping companies, unions, shipyards, City, State and Federal agencies. Captain Harry Allendorfer of the National Trust for Historical Preservation acted as an adviser.

When the work was completed, the hull painted, the repairs and tests of engines and navigational equipment completed, the ship finally sailed on May 21, 1980 and National Liberty Ship Day was proclaimed by President Carter. The ship sailed out of the Golden Gate for a special memorial service for National Maritime Day. Captain Tom Patterson and the San Francisco maritime community leaders then founded The National Liberty Ship Memorial, Inc., a non-profit corporation, and they secured a berth at Fort Mason, San Francisco in the Golden Gate National Recreation Area.

When I came aboard in 1980, it was a nostalgic trip. The ship looked great outwardly. When I visited my old Cadet quarters after 36 years, it was as though I had just left the room and returned to find nothing changed. The built-in furniture was in good shape even though it was not polished, cleaned, or redone. Memories flooded back and brought a tear to my eyes. An unforgettable experience. Deja vu.

Money was and still is a problem. Donations were sorely needed and fund raising was a necessity. Luckily, the National Trust for Historical Preservation granted $5,000,000 in 1992 for marine projects to the 50 states. Full reports had to be written detailing what the monies would be used for; an almost four-inch thick report brought $432,512.00 to the O'Brien, provided the grant could be matched. Another new problem had to be solved, but the hard work of volunteers and those whose love of the sea finally put it all together and earned us the grant to pay the Bethlehem shipyard.

Credit has to be given to all the volunteers and the leadership of the National Liberty Ship Memorial Board of Directors, chaired by Robert Blake.

 # THE LAST CONVOY '94

As early as 1987, at the December Board Meeting of the SS Jeremiah O'Brien, Captain Ernest Murdock submitted to the Board of Directors a proposal, signed by himself and four other volunteers, suggesting that the O'Brien return to Normandy to commemorate the 50th anniversary of the D-Day landings. In November of 1991, Andre del Becq met with the O'Brien leaders to suggest that the ship sail to France to join L'Armada de la Liberte in Rouen.

In April of 1992, John Boylston of Project Liberty Ship SS John W. Brown called a three ship meeting on the Jeremiah O'Brien, with Lane Victory directors Joseph Vernick and Clint Johnson, the staff and directors of the O'Brien, and himself representing the John W. Brown. Mr. Boylston suggested the three ships form a convoy to Normandy, with a Congressional Bill to fund the voyage. This was the beginning of the Last Convoy '94. The convoy would be designated HX 357, the following number after the last convoy of World War II.

The 50th Commemoration of the Anniversary of World War II is an official program of the United States Government. The Department of Defense has been assigned the role of thanking and honoring all World War II veterans, their families and those on the home front, who sacrificed and helped make victory possible. The Last Convoy is part of this commemoration and will be part of all the ceremonies at Normandy. Those aboard these ships will represent all Merchant Mariners from World War II as well as those of today.

The United States Government did encourage the idea of a Last Convoy to commemorate the D-Day events. Congresswoman Helen Bentley and Senators John Breaux and Barbara Mikulski introduced bills in Congress that would enable the ships to acquire funding for repairs for the Normandy Voyage. They were referred to the Committee on Merchant Marine and Fisheries. Bill H.R. 54 was finally signed by President Bush; it provided for the selling of two ships from the Reserve Fleets for scrap for each participating ship. Although the funds helped defray some of the costs, they did not cover all the expenses, and the three ships still had to raise substantial funds on their own.

The plan was to sail from San Francisco, the home port of the Jeremiah O'Brien where the ship is docked at the Fort Mason Center just west of Fisherman's Wharf, and to arrive at Portsmouth, England in time for the D-Day ceremonies. The trip would take upwards of six weeks via the Panama Canal at an average speed of ten knots. After these June 6 ceremonies, she would sail to London and other ports in England and France, then return to the US, where her first stop would be Portland, Maine, where she was launched on June 16, 1943.

The convoy would consist of the three vessels with Admiral Tom Patterson as Commodore. As soon as I had heard of this possibility I made my plans to become part of the crew. Even though 250 volunteers and half of the employed and retired Merchant Mariners on the West Coast wanted to make the voyage, I felt I still had an edge.

I was the only original crew member available for the voyage, having been assigned to the Jeremiah O'Brien as a Cadet/Midshipman for sea training, a part of the course at Kings Point. This was my ace in the hole. You can imagine how disappointed I was when they told me they had all the spaces assigned! I could not accept this and offered my services for any position available. I was finally assigned as assistant steward; now what did that entail? God knows, and I couldn't find out. Specifically, it could be in the galley peeling potatoes or washing dishes, or perhaps serving food or making bunks, or sanitary cleaning. Unfortunately, no one knew, and it would not be known until I met the Steward and was assigned a duty, how it would apply to the above.

Now that I was assigned, I had to start my planning. What part of the voyage would I be allowed to take? I asked for a berth from San Francisco to Portsmouth; surely others would want to sail on the O'Brien and facilities were limited.

The crew that was assigned to the cruise were all volunteers. No one, including the Admiral and the Captain, was receiving any monetary payments. The deck officers included many with licensed Captain's certificates, likewise many in the Engine Department were licensed Chief Engineers.

CHAPTER II

THE VOLUNTEER CREW

The following is a list of the volunteers willing to take the SS Jeremiah O'Brien part or all of the way to D-Day, Normandy and back to San Francisco. The pay is zero, and overtime is paid at the same rate. The hours are when needed, which in the beginning ran as much as 24 hours per day. The work is not easy, it's laborious, and the temperature is hot in the tropics with no air conditioning. However, the food is good and the companionship is fine, even with up to five bunks in a room and doing your own laundry.

The comments are those of the volunteers. Although their histories are not in-depth, each and every one is a fine person and worked well with others in the crew. Morale was great in all departments.

What is great and unique about this voyage is:

- It's the first voyage of an entire volunteer crew selected from over 10,000 volunteers who have given more than 450,000 man-hours that put this ship into excellent shape in the past fourteen years.

- It is the only ship of the 6410 that took part in the invasion of Normandy that is still active and sailed across the Atlantic to commemorate the 1944 landings on Utah and Omaha beaches of Normandy.

- It is the first time a US Merchant Vessel will be part of the "Parade of Ships," with the new Aircraft Carrier the George Washington, the world's largest passenger ship the Queen Elizabeth II, and as many as forty other vessels.

 ## *DECK DEPARTMENT*

The Deck Department consists of up to five licensed Captains at times, each contributing his knowledge to operate the ship at its best. They are willing to serve at any level for the honor of being part of the Normandy voyage of the SS Jeremiah O'Brien.

CAPTAIN
George Jahn, San Francisco, CA

The Captain has been active at sea since 1933 and a master since 1943. He was with the ship when it left the reserve fleet in 1979 and has been a pilot in San Francisco Harbor on all voyages since then. His opinion of the ship is that it is excellent, the best to be chosen from the reserve fleet. That has been proven, since the voyage now completed took the ship over 88,000 miles with no major problems. As captain, his work is commendable, and he is always on call even though he is now approaching 79 years of age. He will be Captain for the entire voyage.

A sweet and gentle person with a friendly smile, he will answer any question any time. He has a good story to tell about the beginning of World War II when he worked for The Matson Steamship Company. His ship was leaving San Francisco on December 1, 1941 for Hawaii. They were told to travel with no lights, blackout the ship. It made no sense to them and they did not blackout. They heard about Pearl Harbor on the 7th and made port in Oahu on the 8th. Their ship, the SS Manini, was a smaller version of the Hog Islander cargo ship. They went to sea again and were torpedoed on Dec. 17, west of Hawaii. The crew took to the two life boats aboard and drifted for ten days. They were off Kauai when they saw an American destroyer and used their last flare, which thankfully brought them rescue. He was also part of a Murmansk convoy.

ADMIRAL
Thomas Patterson, San Rafael, CA Kings Point 1944
Commodore and Voyage Chairman for D-Day celebrations for the Jeremiah O'Brien

He served first on Merchant Vessels, then in 1950 was Navy-bound and became Captain of the USS Agri Guardian and James G Squires. He retired from the Navy in 1957 and became Maritime Administrator of the West Coast.

Admiral Patterson was the primary person in selecting the Jeremiah O'Brien as a possible Liberty Ship to save as a memorial of World War II. It was the least altered ship at the reserve fleet in Suisun Bay. It was original in all respects, as if it had just come from the launching ways. After all, it had only sailed for two and a half years before being placed in the National Defense Reserve Fleet. He is due credit for the organization, enthusiasm, and spirit that turned this rusting hulk ready for the scrap heap into a National Memorial of which any Merchant Mariner who sailed on any of the 2751 ships built from 1942 to 1945 could be proud. It also honors the American labor that put this ship together in 56 days and did more than many to bring victory to the Western world.

FIRST MATE
Walter Jaffee, Benicia, CA Kings Point 1965

The Chief mate also has his Master's License and has been active for many years as a volunteer. He teaches part-time at the California Maritime Academy. Walter has written a number of books:The Last T-2 Tanker, The Lane Victory and the Last Liberty Ship, the SS Jeremiah O'Brien. I hear his typewriter singing, so you can expect a sequel to that last book:The Last Liberty Ship, the voyage to Normandy. His books are complete and technically correct as well as interesting. The Chief mate will make the complete voyage.

SECOND MATE
Raymond Conrady, San Francisco, CA

Ray has been sailing since 1965. He has been a volunteer for the past two years. When he was interviewed, he accepted the position as second mate. Ray says it's like a busman's holiday. They have had no problems on the bridge, except with the new equipment. All the old stuff works fine. There are 2 GPS units on board, besides a radar and satellite transmitter, both on loan to the ship.

He was also giving the weather and position of the ship daily, as well as information about the crew, via a special phone message center in San Francisco. My, how easy things have become! Ray is one for the full trip.

THIRD MATE
Peter Knute Lyse, Menominee, MI

He attended college from 1949 to 1954, earning a degree from Leheigh University in Civil Engineering. From 1956 to 1959, he served with the US Coast Guard, and he still remains in the reserve. He has his Great Lakes Pilot license from Duluth to Gary and Buffalo. In 1989 he sailed two Liberty Colliers.

Peter was originally to be 3rd Mate on the John W. Brown but was called by the Jeremiah O'Brien when it was realized that the Brown would not make the voyage. He left the ship in Portsmouth, England and finds her better than he expected; the trip was a real bonus.

THIRD MATE
William Dickerson, Seattle, WA

Bill came aboard at Portsmouth, England, to relieve Peter Lyse. He claims it is a busman's holiday, since he will have to return to his ship; this is only a working vacation. He enjoyed one of Jim Farras' famous birthday cakes.

BOSUN
Richard Reed, Novato, CA

Rich has been a captain of a San Francisco pilot boat for the past 15 years. He has been a volunteer for 13 years. He's the kind of guy who generates respect, a true leader because he knows what he's doing. He calls this voyage a holiday.

KINGS POINT CADET, Deck
Nathan Taylor, Weatherford, TX

Nate always loved the water and used to spend many hours on the Brazas River in Texas. As a cadet, he has already sailed on the President Washington, an APL C-9 container ship. His grandfather sailed on a Liberty Ship, and he wanted to learn seamanship on old and well as new vessels. He wishes to make the Merchant Marine his career and is proud of the service. He feels this is the privilege of a lifetime.

Nate was accepted at West Point, Annapolis, and the Merchant Marine Academy. He says he chose the USMMA because it offered the best education of all the schools.

DECK ENGINEER
William Duncan, Alameda, CA

Bill was in the Army during WWII and was aboard a Liberty Ship upon his return from overseas. He spent 32 years in the Army and has been a volunteer for seven years and is crew chairman. His family includes an uncle and father who were both Chief Engineers. He is taking the voyage for nostalgic reasons and to visit the graves of friends who lost their lives on an LST on D-Day at Normandy.

DECK ENGINEER
Edward Smith, Pacifica, CA

Ed has been a volunteer for 2 years. He was an Oiler, FWT, and Electrician at sea from 1943 until 1951. He is very happy with the ship's performance; "Can't beat it," he says. Every problem has been minor and you will always find him with a smile.

ABLE BODIED SEAMAN AB
William Russel Bennett, Vallejo, CA

He has already volunteered three years on the Jeremiah O'Brien, enough to be a welcome volunteer on the entire voyage from SF to home again.
Bill loves this ship. You can call on him for anything. He spent 22 years in the Coast Guard and feels this is a necessary trip for the pride of the United States. At home, Bill has a wife and eight children waiting for the story of his experiences.

ABLE BODIED SEAMAN AB
James Conwell, Sacramento, CA

Jim has been a volunteer for nine years and was quickly accepted for the Normandy cruise. He feels the pain and hard work was paid for the second day

the ship was out of San Francisco. He is so happy with the ship and its promise of a great voyage that he loves every day aboard.

ABLE BODIED SEAMAN AB
James Miller, San Francisco, CA

Jim was an insurance underwriter before he joined the volunteers on the O'Brien in 1983 and had donated between 4000 and 5000 hours before the voyage started. He is thrilled to have been selected to join the voyage.

ABLE BODIED SEAMAN AB
Philip Sinnott, Lafayette, CA

Phil sailed for two years with ATS, and has been a volunteer since 1980. He thinks it is a great trip, worth all the effort and work it has cost beyond question. He will be aboard for part of the voyage.

ABLE BODIED SEAMAN AB
Marty Wefald, San Francisco, CA

He sailed from 1947 to 1957 as an AB. He has also sailed on the John W. Brown from Portland to San Francisco. Marty has been a volunteer for the past two years. He will be aboard for the whole voyage. Time is moving too fast, he claims, and he needs the voyage to sort things out.

ORDINARY SEAMAN
Samuel Wood, San Francisco, CA

He sailed as AB for Farrell Lines from 1965 to 1971, and he volunteered in 1993 as a carpenter for the Fort Mason Foundation. He saw the story of the O'Brien in the newspaper and wondered if he could make the voyage, and is delighted for the opportunity.

ORDINARY SEAMAN
Joseph Callahan, Sacramento, CA

Joe signed up for deck training in 1943 and was sent to the Maritime school at Sheepshead Bay, where he was issued an AB ticket. He sailed with the Army Transport Command. In 1944 he was assigned Yeoman, then Purser on the USS Sea Cat. In December 1945, he retired from the sea and was employed by Pacific Telephone. Joe came aboard the O'Brien in 1992 as a volunteer and joined the voyage immediately.

The trip is an excursion of curiosity and adventure, a voyage into the past, a time capsule, and it shows the 'can do' of the 40's generation. His last comment to me was, "We may meet some day in that great forecastle in the sky," as I was departing from Panama. He sailed part of the voyage to Portsmouth, England and returned home.

ORDINARY SEAMAN
Michael Emery, Petaluma, CA

Mike is the camera man, shooting hundreds of photos almost daily. He is a recruit and serving as ordinary seaman as well as photographer. He believes it is a good story and waited two months before being accepted. He's amazed we left San Francisco but is sold on what the ship can do. He shot 300 rolls of film and developed them all himself. Mike is planning two major exhibitions in San Francisco and has the best collection of photographs of anyone on the ship.

Part of his work will be shown in a booklet to be produced by the San Francisco Chronicle on Sept. 23, 1994.

ORDINARY SEAMAN
Bruce McMurtry, San Francisco, CA

He was in the Navy and served on the USS Boston CAG1, the Constellation, Ranger, Carl Vincent, and Abraham Lincoln as Bosun's mate and 1st class master at arms, then joined the Coast Guard Reserve for three and a half years. He is now in the Naval Reserve.

Bruce was a volunteer for 6 months before agreeing to make the voyage, which he considers a trip into history.

ORDINARY SEAMAN
Martin Shields, San Francisco, CA

Marty was a paint contractor from Cleveland. While on an eight-week vacation in San Francisco, he was offered the opportunity to make the Voyage to D-Day. The Jeremiah O'Brien provided him a chance to collect his time toward his 3rd Mate's License; he already held a Captain's license for vessels of fifty tons on the Great Lakes. Marty is thrilled to death because this voyage could happen only once in a lifetime. It is a trip of trips and the center of activities for this time in history. He will be aboard for the entire voyage.

ORDINARY SEAMAN
William Rowlands

He was always there when needed and gave interviews and good explanations to Navy reporters. Bill took the whole voyage.

ORDINARY SEAMAN
Jean Yates, Sebastopol, CA

During WWII he was with Chanault and made thirty missions in a B-25. Since then, he has been an art teacher at Santa Rosa Jr. College for twenty-two years. He's also a great train buff and brought almost 100 videos of his own on board for the crew to use.
Jean has been a volunteer for six and a half years. He often visits the ship. He will leave her in Le Harve.

CARPENTER and AB
Robert Burnett, Redwood City, CA

It seems he never stops working; this eight year volunteer is always at something. Just ask for a carpenter's problem to be solved and he will be there. His greatest pride is in restoring everything on the ship to its 1943 position and look, but don't just add something without giving

23

it a lot of forethought or you're in trouble! He is a deep water sailor and has sailed to Hawaii in a small sailing boat. He is also an engineer at an aeronautics plant.

Bob will be on board for the entire trip. He says it's the historical voyage of a lifetime.

UTILITY
Francois Le Pendu, San Francisco, CA

Our Frenchman is a two-year volunteer. He writes out phrases in French on the crew mess blackboard for our trip to France.

Francois served nine years in the French Navy and was an engineer in the Merchant Marine aboard a diesel ship. He feels the ship is in good shape and never thought he would get a chance to make the voyage. He will leave us in Le Harve.

UTILITY
Carl Note, Pearl Heights, CA

Carl is aboard as a reporter for the San Francisco Chronicle and has sent news and location stories by fax almost daily; they are very interesting and informative. He has a Monterey 26' boat, so he is no stranger to the sea. Because of Carl, the ship received almost daily publicity on the West Coast through the medium of the San Francisco Chronicle, something it needed because many other areas of the country were not as informed.

He says it has been a great trip on a historic ship, and he loves to travel and says there isn't a train he wouldn't take. He was on and off making parts of the voyage.

ENGINEERING DEPT.

The engineering department is made up of crew members and officers who together have more skill, knowledge, and information on one ship than some five Liberty Ships had during World War II. The licensed officers, many with Chief Engineer's licenses, are taking available positions for the honor of sailing on the SS Jeremiah O'Brien to Normandy and back.

CHIEF ENGINEER
Dick Brannon, Pacifica, CA Graduate of California Maritime Academy and Kings Point 1940.

Dick has been to sea since 1935, he will never quit. His life is the engine room; he worries and nurtures his engines. He calls this a repeat voyage of the Jean Applegate, a Liberty Ship on which he once sailed. He agrees that the morale is superb. He will make the entire trip.

FIRST ASSISTANT ENGINEER
Stephen Worthy, Walnut Creek, CA

Steve has been at sea for 30 years starting at the bottom as wiper, then oiler and fireman, right up to first engineer. He began sailing when he was seventeen years old and is a graduate of the California Maritime Academy. His father sailed on a Liberty during WWII.

Steve feels this voyage is a cruise of a lifetime, and he could not pass up the experience and a payback to the Maritime industry. He is making the first stage of the voyage to Panama.

SECOND ASSISTANT ENGINEER
Tim Palange, Palmetto, CA who will become First Assistant Engineer when Stephen Worthy leaves in Panama

Tim spent seven years in the Navy as an electrician; he was offered chief petty office and refused to become a First Assistant in the Merchant Marine. He will make the whole trip. To him, the voyage represents an unparalleled piece of living history, he said he would quit his job just to make this trip.

THIRD ASSISTANT ENGINEER
James Gillis, Millbrae, CA

He has been to sea all his working life and retired in 1983. He has been a volunteer on the O'Brien. Unfortunately, he was not prepared for the 50-year old ship with the wartime uncomfortable bunks, the oppressive heat, the hot, dirty, and greasy steam engines. Most of his time was spent as Chief Engineer. He wanted to get this out of his system, one more voyage on a steam ship.

THIRD ASSISTANT ENGINEER
Hans Miller, San Francisco, CA

He has been a volunteer since 1982, sailed as ordinary in 1985. He attended Great Lakes Maritime School and graduated a 3rd Engineer in 1990. He has enjoyed the cruise even with the hard work required and claims the learning experience has been fun. This has represented his action time and he must leave to go back to work from Panama. His father manned a mine sweeper in the US Navy during the D-Day invasion. Hans is employed by the Port of Oakland, Ca.

KINGS POINT CADET, Engine
Dirk Warren, Waldorf, MD

From Kings Point, Dirk was assigned to the container ship Sea Lane Tacoma; then he received an offer from Captain Donald Davenport to volunteer for the Liberty Ship Jeremiah O'Brien, which he readily accepted. While waiting for the ship to sail he was assigned to the Keystone Golden Gate coastwide tanker. He has been an asset to the engine room starting as an oiler. He enjoys the Jeremiah O'Brien's reciprocating engines, learning basic steam. He loves the trip and will stay to Le Harve, then back to Kings Point to complete his education.

FIREMAN, WATER TENDER FWT
Robert Noisseux, Plainfield, CT

An early graduate of Kings Point 1994 sailing as a fireman but licensed as a Third Engineer, he took the latter post when the crew changed at Panama. He advanced his graduation by about four months by taking 30 credits in the last two years. The reason for the early completion of his studies was to go to sea on the Jeremiah O'Brien. His hobby is old machinery and he is now making a movie about the Jeremiah's engine and fire room equipment, to be shown September 13 at a gathering of naval architects.

His experience with old machinery was proven when no one on board could get the lifeboat engines going; in a matter of two hours he helped us get the two troublesome engines running as smoothly as if they had just been purchased and installed.

FIREMAN, WATER TENDER FWT
Richard Currie, Saratoga, CA

Richard was in the Coast Guard for eight and a half years and is still in the reserves. He has been a volunteer for the past two and a half years and sees the voyage as a once-in-a-lifetime adventure.

FIREMAN, WATER TENDER FWT
Alex Hochstraser, Pacifica, CA

Alex has been a volunteer since November 1993, and this is his first voyage to sea. His father was active in the French underground and was captured and imprisoned, then escaped on D-Day. He became an FWT and sailed on a Liberty Ship for 2 years. Alex loves the trip and finds it wonderful.

FIREMAN, WATER TENDER FWT
Edgar Lingonfeld, Redwood,CA

Edgar served during WWII from 1943 till 1947 and in Korea from 1951 to 1954. He has also served as an Oiler and 3rd Assistant. He has given the Jeremiah O'Brien four years of volunteer service. He wanted to make this his last voyage.

OILER
Gene Anderson, San Jose, CA

Gene sailed on a Liberty ship in 1945 for three years. He has been a volunteer for thirteen years. This nostalgic cruise, he feels, is the last of a lifetime, a good way to finish life. Meanwhile, he is enjoying every minute aboard the Jeremiah O'Brien.

OILER
Norman Burke, Los Gatos, CA

Norman sailed as oiler, FWT, and electrician on Liberty ships and Tankers during WWII. He went ashore when he had to assist his father in business.

Norman has a sympathetic ear and sensors for large machinery and understands them well. He knows the engineers of the Jeremiah O'Brien are experts well beyond the requirements of the ship and has no fears of any major problems arising.

He left in Panama but will be available if required anywhere the O'Brien travels. Norm has been a volunteer since 1979.

OILER
William Concannon, Portland, OR

Bill is a licensed Fireman FWT and has gone to sea for over a year. While on vacation he visited the ship with his brother, who mentioned the D-Day voyage coming up. He was very enthusiastic and said he would give his eyetooth to make the voyage to Portsmouth. Luckily, it hasn't come to that.

OILER
Richard A. Phill, South San Francisco, CA

An active oiler at sea for eight years and a volunteer for five years, he admits he has never been as hot in any engine room as on this voyage. While sailing down the West Coast of Mexico at the start of the voyage, the temperatures in the engine room rose to 130 degrees with extremely high humidity. All of the engineers, FWT, Oilers, and Wipers survived.

He will be aboard until Le Harve.

OILER
Dennis Rodd, Benici, CA

Dennis joined the ship in Panama. He worked on steamships in the northwest and in Canada for five years. He sailed a cutter from Oxward,

Ca. to New Zealand and returned to Seattle. He is a two-year volunteer and will make the trip from Panama to London.

WIPER
Arnold Sears, San Francisco, CA

He has his FWT card but has no sea experience. He has been a volunteer for two years and really wanted to make the voyage on the Jeremiah O'Brien. He will stay aboard till Portland, ME. He loves to talk and reminisce about the ship.

WIPER
Mary Steinberg, Mill Valley, CA

Our only young lady aboard, she has also been struggling with the heat but puts up a good front. She was also a volunteer for two years; she feels the voyage is fine and gave it an OK. Being the only woman on board was not an easy situation for Mary, and she left in Portsmouth, England.

PURSER

PURSER
James Wade, San Leandro, CA

Our Purser and Chaplain served at a Scotland Naval Base near Glasgow as a hospital corpsman in 1943, where unbeknownst to him and me we crossed paths as the Jeremiah O'Brien stopped for repairs on her first return voyage directly across from the Hospital.

He is a volunteer thrilled with the chance of reunion with WWII veterans, as well as satisfying his love for the sea.

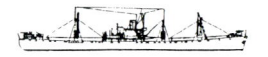

RADIO OPERATOR

RADIO
Robert Gisslow, San Francisco, CA

Bob sailed from 1943 until 1946 as a radio operator. Looking at all the equipment of the 1943 radios, which filled two sides of the radio shack, in comparison to the little radio now required, which measures about 10" x 6" x 10" and has twice the power of the older models, is awe-inspiring. We even have a fax machine receiving from radio transmissions; it's all miraculous.

Bob is the kind of gentleman who is only too happy to assist anyone with patched-in direct phone calls, connections, or messages in or out. He loves the voyage and will be there till the end.

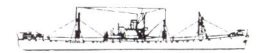

SHIP'S DOCTOR

SHIP'S DOCTOR
Kenneth Haslam, Chestertown, MD

Ken first went to sea as doctor on a Russian ice breaker to the Arctic, then later on two trips with larger Russian ice breakers to the Antarctic. Ken was all set to be aboard the SS John W. Brown as doctor, requested by the Coast Guard. After a holiday in New Zealand, he stopped in San Francisco to see Doctor Frank Nelson, who was assigned to the SS Jeremiah O'Brien, to determine what medical supplies would be required on the Brown. Some days later, he was informed of the Brown's decision not to make the voyage to Normandy. He immediately phoned Frank Nelson and learned the US Navy would not allow Nelson to be doctor aboard the O'Brien. The decision for Ken to come to San Francisco was made immediately; Ken would be the Ship's Doctor for the O'Brien.

He arrived the morning of the 14th and set up the hospital. Dr. Ken will attend the ceremonies of D-Day and join the cruise into history. For my sake, thank God he was aboard! He will make the whole voyage back to San Francisco.

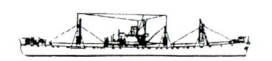

STEWARD'S DEPT.

CHIEF STEWARD
Russel Mosholder, San Leandro, CA

Russ was a Navy man in 1942 for three years, later he owned restaurants and was active as a caterer. He was a volunteer and asked to be steward. He has a tough job and a lot of responsibility. To him the voyage is great, a love, challenge, and choice of a lifetime, the last hurrah.

Author, John Carraher, Pat McCafferty, and Russ Mosholder.

ASSISTANT STEWARD
Coleman 'Coke' Schneider, Tenafly, NJ (Author)

Kings Point 1944, licensed Second Mate, and New York Harbor Pilot 1st Class Unlimited tonnage. Original cadet aboard the Jeremiah O'Brien, assigned to the ship in Boston July 15, 1943, sailed for nine months making four round trips (counted as Voyages 1-2-3) across the North Atlantic. Returning to the ship for nostalgic reasons, I asked how many people got a chance to relive their nineteenth year on the same ship across the same ocean 50 years later. I was to leave the ship in Portsmouth, but, concerned for the finances of the ship, I left in Panama to raise funds to secure oil so she could complete the voyage and make stops at major cities on the East coast on the return voyage.

I returned to the ship in Portsmouth and was asked to come aboard again to make the voyage to Normandy. I left the ship again in Chatham, England.

CHIEF COOK
Allen Martino, San Rafael, CA

Soft spoken Al started his sea time in the US Navy as radar man and also spent twenty-three years as a San Francisco fireman. He became a volunteer in 1993 and hoped to come aboard to get back to sea again and to Normandy. The chief cook's job is the same at sea as well as in port. They all put in up to sixteen hours per day without complaint.

Al will be aboard for the entire voyage.

SECOND COOK
James Farras, Daly City, CA

He is a graduate of the Marine Cooks and Stewards School, which turns out the best for which the Merchant Marine has always been known. He has gone to sea for eight and a half years. His first sight of the Jeremiah O'Brien was during a lunch at Fort Mason. The gangway was down, and he walked aboard and asked about the coming voyage. He spoke to Captain George Jahn, who asked what kind of baker he was. He replied, "I can bake with my eyes closed." That he has verified without a doubt!

Jimmy said he fell in love with the ship and volunteered.

THIRD COOK
Eduardo Pubill, San Francisco, CA

He spent one year on the Windjammer Fatome in 1971, he loves volunteer work and was accepted as 3rd cook for the full voyage.

He knows the voyage will be a historical moment in his life and wants to make the stops at Normandy on D-Day.

MESSMAN
Patrick McCafferty, San Francisco, CA

As chief messman Pat has the most experience in the art of messman, spending more than thirty years at sea on various cruise ships, where he was also slop chest director. He adds a certain class to the job and feels a great affinity for the Merchant Service. He will be aboard for the entire cruise.

MESSMAN
Ronald Smith, Portland, OR

Ron has had an RV home for twenty years; he loves to travel. Originally from Chicago, he joined as a messman with no experience. Ron has spent twenty years of his life in the US Air Force and is now retired. He is a three-year volunteer and has always wanted to go to sea. He has a great admiration for WWII veterans and wants to share in their reunion. He will be part of the steward's department until he reaches Southampton, when he transfers to the Armed Guard.

MESSMAN
Rudolph Arelland, Redway, CA

He was an active Merchant Mariner in 1943-44 and in the Army until 1946. He went to sea again in 1950 and has served on a Liberty ship. He has been a volunteer since September 1993. Rudy received an invitation in May and wanted to come along and join in the adventure when he heard we were going to commemorate D-Day and honor the Merchant Marine.

Rudy is a hard worker, putting in the required hours in the galley without complaints, the type of person that makes the SS Jeremiah O'Brien a great ship.

MESSMAN
John Carraher, Monterey Park, CA

John was employed by the San Pedro Steam vessels, spent three years in the Army, and retired after being employed in L.A. County as inspector in the road department. He now teaches English as a second language. He chose to make the trip because he was a history major in college and was an SS Jeremiah O'Brien volunteer and wanted to live the adventure.

He does lead the crew at times in sea chanteys. You can also hear him announcing the mess calls with his little chimes.

UTILITY
Greg Williams, Elmira, CA

Greg spent two years in the Navy aboard the USS Grandville S Hall. He was involved in technical research. He has been a volunteer aboard the Jeremiah O'Brien for seven years, acting as a carpenter. He applied and was accepted for the full voyage.

He also assisted the doctor with his Pharmaceutical experience.

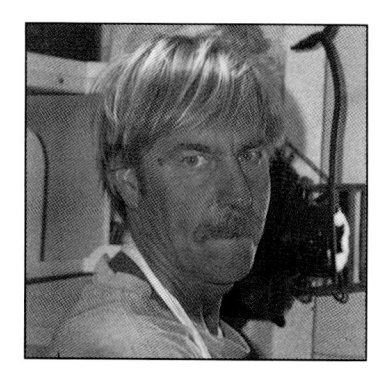

US NAVY ARMED GUARD

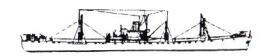

CHIEF GUNNER (USN)
Carl Kreidler, San Lorenxo, CA

Carl was in the US Navy from May 1942 until April 1946 in the Armed Guard on Merchant Ships and nine months on a destroyer. He's a married man with 3 children who encouraged him to make the voyage. As a volunteer, his job is to keep the guns in shape, although they can not be fired and no ammunition is aboard. Carl says the trip so far is fantastic and will be with us to London.

He was asked to return to Portland, Maine, but when he got there a new Armed Guard person was already assigned so he returned home.

GUNNER'S MATE
Otto Sommerauer, San Francisco, CA

He was born in Switzerland and came to the US in 1953. Otto was active in the Swiss Air Force and knew many Americans who came to Switzerland after the war to attend college. When he came to the US, he was employed by the Municipal railway in San Francisco. He saw an ad for volunteers for the Jeremiah O'Brien and quickly joined. He left the ship to visit Switzerland and old friends again.

CHAPTER III

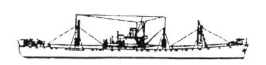

COMING ABOARD

April 11, 1994

I left Newark Airport at 8:30 AM on the 11th, kissing my wife goodbye and feeling some apprehension at the coming six weeks of sea duty. I arrived at noon and the first call was to find out where the ship was; she was at the San Francisco dry dock. Upon coming aboard the O'Brien, I stepped into a beehive of activity. People were climbing all over the ship, sparks flew from welders, cables were strewn all over, the Coast Guard was here with the Navy and the American Bureau of Shipping. All were lending a helping hand.

Russ the steward immediately assigned me to straighten out the linen closet, which contained all the linens, waiters' jackets, towels, sheets, blankets and pillows, etc. It did not take long.

Piles of linens were contaminated with mildew; these would be discarded. They had been picked up from a Victory Ship at the reserve fleet in Suison Bay and loaded into an open truck, where a rain storm soaked them, and naturally they had been stored in the same condition.

ABC television was aboard to do interviews for "Good Morning America" and most of the day was devoted to them. One job still pending was moving four or five canvas cots out of the storage rooms. They were to be used for sleeping on deck in the hot climates we would encounter. Four or five turned out to be over 200, moved to the main deck for storage in hold #3.

The cooks are great! We had a terrific turkey dinner, with a dessert of rice pudding. That night I made my bunk and took a cold water shower. There was no hot water, as the fuses had failed; terrible, since it was a hot sweaty day. I settled in after an eighteen-hour day of traveling and working. The night was very cold and I started looking for blankets but never got back to sleep.

Getting the ship ready took many dedicated people several hours into the night to accomplish what was required.

April 12, 1994

The breakfast was invigorating and I asked Russ for something to do. This was the day that all the food supplies for 56 crew members for six months would arrive. Space had to be made in the storerooms to categorize the foods on the deck below. I moved about 50 cases of beer out of one storeroom into another and then the French television crew was aboard and wanted interviews. This took about four hours, and I never got back to any kind of constructive work to prepare the ship for departure. The boxed food arrived around noon, and many people including ship yard volunteers helped to move it from the main deck to a lower one and stack these hundreds of cartons in dry, cooled, and frozen storage.

Corned beef and cabbage was on the menu tonight, great cooks!

Many crew members are still going to devote time this evening to complete jobs before we can leave the ship yard.

The word is out that the ship will move about 10 AM to Pier 35 at Fisherman's Wharf. This is good news since it would be impossible to move the ship without the permission of the Coast Guard, so the final sailing will be set for Thursday at noon... we assume.

April 13, 1994

Food stores lined the dock, the dock cranes lifted it to the deck, naturally on the wrong side of the ship. Then, with the assistance of three dock workers and those free from other duties, we brought the cartons on hand trucks through the main deck alleyway and slid them to the lower deck for storage. You can't imagine the amount of food to be stored for so few people. It seemed like a full train load.

We learned that the ship would not be ready to depart on Thursday and more work was required for an oil leak in hold #3. But something had to be done since all the contributors and volunteer workers were to have their grand bon voyage party on Pier 35 at 4 PM. Conferences took place with the Admiral and Captain and Coast Guard officers, and the decision was made to move the ship to Pier 35 for the event, then return to the shipyard in the morning to complete the work.

The party was attended by hundreds of well wishers, and food and drink was plentiful and free. Visitors were allowed aboard and hundreds came. Speeches were made by attendees including the British and French consuls and various companies that made substantial contributions to the costs of the voyage. Admiral Tom Patterson was the master of ceremonies and introduced all of the dignitaries and original crew who were joining the voyage. By this time I had counted eight interviews with various radio, TV, and magazine journalists and book authors. The party lasted until about 8 PM.

April 14, 1994

At 7 AM we are supposed to shift to the shipyard from pier 35 for completion of required repairs before we can be off to Portsmouth. We knew it wouldn't be today, but hopefully we can set sail within the next two days.

We just received the sad news that The Liberty Ship John W. Brown will not make the voyage because of a shortage of funds for rivet repairs in the hull. Naturally the next question was, can the Lane Victory make the voyage? The word at this time is that if they can't start by the 18th of April, they too will not make the convoy. The cost for all three ships is unbelievable and most of it has been raised by the ships themselves. Unfortunately, we are working with ships built to comply with 1942 regulations, and 1994 regulations are being applied.

Boat drill was sounded about 10:30 AM for approval by the Coast Guard; this was the second drill this week, and we performed better than the first time. The boats were lowered and the men had to climb down about 50 feet on the Jacob's ladder, get into position in the boat, and set the oars to row in a wide circle. They then stored the oars and stepped the mast and set sail. The drill lasted about three and a half hours and was finally sanctioned by the inspectors.

"Good Morning America" was aboard to tape their Sunday show; this was the tenth group to interview and film the ship. We all lined up on the port forward deck, the Admiral made a statement: "This is the last Liberty Ship and will make a voyage to D-Day as it did in 1944," then there was a loud cheer of "Good Morning America!"

Work continued through the night as required projects were brought to completion.

April 15, 1994

Stores were brought aboard, a leak was discovered in #2 hold, and the Coast Guard made it very plain that "this ship does not leave this dock until the problem is solved." The problems were very much in our minds, but we hoped we could leave by Saturday.

The ship is light in the water and must add ballast. Water is added to tanks not being used for fuel, and tons of anchor chain are being stowed in #2 hatch, shored so it stays in one place. Containers of lead are lowered into #1.

April 16, 1994

The day started with a tremendous amount of work for everyone. We all felt we had to get the job done so we could start the voyage to Europe. Jack Sisson from MARAD, the Captain, and the Admiral called a meeting of all department heads for 1000 hours. Jack had made a list of all that had to be completed before the ship would be allowed to sail. Each of the items required the approval of the Coast Guard, the American Bureau of Shipping, or the FCC for radio gear.

The list was comprised of 72 items, many of them major, and the problems were equally spread between the deck and engine departments. The list was read item for item to find the status of each uncompleted task. The answers were to be 0% (nothing accomplished), 25%, 50%, 75%, or signed off as completed by one of the agencies.

Much work had to be done and the heads were advised to check each problem and report for another get-together at 1400 hours. for a status report. The same procedures were applied again and a number of items were signed off. Another meeting was called for 1800 hours. Again the same questions were asked, and the forceful Mr. Sisson made his point.

April 17, 1994

Sunday arrived with many of the same problems, though many had been completed and it seemed safe to assume the ship could sail by Monday. There was scuttlebutt that the Lane Victory could join us in the convoy, and also rumors that she could not, for lack of funds.

More stores arrived for the steward's department. We received three pallets of beer but had no idea who had sent them, so who was to receive this? The Chief Steward was so upset, he warned that if anyone caught drinking beer would be put off the ship, but the Captain told us to store the beer along with the champagne and wine in the cooler in #4.

An extra effort from the crew was exerted to meet approval for the remaining items. The dock crew from the San Francisco dry dock put in the time to assist us in correcting those deficiencies because they wanted to see us off as well.

April 18, 1994

This is the day we are to leave the dock at 12 noon. Jobs required by the Coast Guard are still being inspected and, thankfully, approved.

As the time approaches people began to flood onto the dock for the goodbye wave, reminding one of seeing off your son to war.

One more interview by ABC was being conducted while the gangway was secured. This was my seventeenth interview. Finally, the

Coke Schneider giving last interview with Phil Hay of BBC before sailing.

ABC reporter and cameraman came aboard along with some special guests, Coast Guard inspectors, ABS inspectors, the pilot and those setting the compass .

The lines were let go about ten minutes after noon and you could feel the gentle movement of the ship and she steamed very slowly from the dock to cheers of good luck and safe passage from hundreds of well-wishers. The San Francisco Fire Boat was escorting us along with her fire hoses at full pressure, sending us off with red, white and blue streams of water.

Daily reports became available to anyone who wanted information on the ship's position and daily routines. This was achieved by calling a specific number in San Francisco. Contacting the ship was also possible throughout the long voyage by contacting KFS World Communications in San Francisco where you could FAX or speak to those aboard.

AT SEA

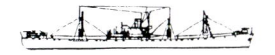

APRIL 18, 1994

    The first day at sea. After we passed under the Golden Gate Bridge, we sailed out about five miles to start the tests for compass, that is, to check for deviation at all compass points. Ship trials for the boilers and other boiler room equipment also took place. Water pressure tests for leaks into the cargo holds took place on deck. A pilot boat followed us for two hours, waiting for the final approvals. As those leaving the ship gathered on the forward deck, the Captain made the final announcement, "We have been approved on all points and will now sail for Portsmouth, England." A huge hurrah sounded from the crew as we assisted the inspectors down the Jacob's ladder to the waiting Pilot boat. When the last passengers were gone, the engine telegraph rang "full speed ahead" and we were on our way to Portsmouth.

    The gentle roll of the Jeremiah O'Brien put us all at ease. We were in dense fog but on our way. Many seamen came on deck to see the beautiful rolling ocean, the quietness, the expanse and wonder of it all. We knew everyone would sleep well this evening and listen to the throbbing of the engines.

April 19, 1994

The seas were calm, and everyone was surprised by the speed of the ship; we were traveling over thirteen knots per hour with the assistance of the currents, winds, and tides; the best we had expected was eight or nine knots. We felt the extra speed was because of the clean bottom just out of the ship yard, and the IFO60 fuel which the engines consumed at a rate of seven BBL per hour.

    It was a working day for all, setting our routines for the voyage, cleaning the decks, and still doing the odds and ends as needed. We sailed not more than twenty-five miles off the California coast as sanctioned by the US Coast Guard. As we approached Southern California we followed the channel between the mainland and Catalina island, passing a few large container ships heading north.

Since we do not have any AC power for the TVs in #2 hold, we used the stewards' TV in the officers' mess and watched "The Cruel Sea," which I had brought along after checking that no one else had.

What's this thing I'm sitting on? A wallet with credit cards? When will I need this again? Not soon, so I packed it away for another day.

April 20, 1994

Another beautiful day with a slight roll. Still getting organized. The engine department set three-hour watches in anticipation of the hot weather which will arrive when we sail deeper into the tropics.

We have 500 VCR films aboard, and two new large screen videos have been loaned to us by Norway House, a San Francisco seafarers' organization. The ship is set up with DC current and anything plugged into DC that should be AC will burn up, so we need a special AC line for the two TV's. I asked for the privilege of setting up the programs so we can show four films per night, at 6:15 for the earlier watch in the engine room and at 8:15 for the 4 to 8 deck watch.

Only beautiful sea and sky to see, two sailboats sailing north came and went.

April 21, 1994

Richard Brannon, the Chief Engineer, is someone who looks at, feels, and nurtures his engines; it is the most important part of the voyage to him, his tunnel vision seeing only those reciprocating engines turning over smoothly. The engines were designed for 76 revolutions and are running smoothly at 67. No one aboard need worry about the propulsion part of this voyage.

It was time to let everyone know where we were, so I set up a chart on the alleyway outside the mess halls. I will be marking the ship's position every day at noon. We have been averaging twelve knots constantly, a minimum of 250 nautical miles per day. We asked the captain why we were making such good progress and he explained that we were running down hill.

Daily chores are catching up with the mess caused by the shipyard; decks have been washed, and grease and oil on the deck is being cleaned with tooth brushes, the only way to get into the welds.

The idea for four movies per night can not be achieved since a 1900 show is as late as anyone wants to attend. Now we are only using one TV on the new connection set up by the electricians.

April 22, 1994

Sausage and pancakes this breakfast, our second cook is some good baker! Fire and boat drill scheduled for 1030, not necessary to lower the boats, so everyone is in their life vest at their stations and heads are counted. This was to have been a Friday call every week from here on in, but it never happened.

General routine was the order of the day. Seamen usually work an eight-hour day; if the day is longer there is overtime to consider. However, in this case, with volunteers there is no time limit on work, and all of us want the ship in its best condition on arrival in Portsmouth, therefore work has no time limit.

As we approached Cabo San Lucas the views were terrific. You could see all the hotels but could not find the small airfield I landed in about ten years ago. The place has grown tremendously. A beautiful evening and sunset.

April 23, 1994

    The deck department schedule of four on and four off works well, new AB's at the wheel have gotten the feel of the helm and you can feel it in choppy seas as well as smooth.

    We are still clipping along at twelve knots. The weather is getting warmer and a little exertion starts you sweating. Saturday is normally a day off at sea for the deck crew, but it seems since we are all volunteers, the work just continues.

    We have tried to show movies in #2 hold but the heat is tremendous. About fifteen showed up for "Action in the North Atlantic" with Humphrey Bogart and Raymond Massey. I scheduled a second movie but no one showed. Many are on watch and we are trying to time the two features so those going on watch and coming off watch will be able to see one of the movies.

    Don't forget, we are traveling in a steel box and close to having the sun overhead, a porthole is not enough for air especially if you are on the leeward side of the ship.

April 24, 1994

    Today being Sunday, the Padre (who is also the Purser) is holding services for Protestants at 0900 and Catholics at 1000. There are about three Jews on board but he is not an authorized Rabbi. From 7:30 breakfast service the time passed quickly and thank God, the #2 hold where the services were held was not hot at this time. The heat is becoming unbearable and the Steward just brought out a case of beer, which lightened our spirits (at least it was cold!).

    Great dinner for all tonight; steak, baked potatoes, cucumber and onion salad with cauliflower and rolls topped off with rice pudding.

    Tonight was our first chance to show two movies, but this time on deck, on #2 hatch. We had one TV facing port and one starboard. The movies drew about fifteen on each side, "Patton" and "Tora Tora."

April 25, 1994

Breakfast was the normal pancakes and sausage, grapefruit or melon and cold grape juice. We finally got the steward to call a meeting of the nine of us in the stewards department for better organization. There was a lot of grumbling, but he listened carefully, made some changes and all were satisfied.

Porpoises were playing around the bow, swimming twelve knots in front of the ship, dozens of small ones, jumping out of the water until they gave up the game and swam away. There were also plenty of flying fish skipping over the waves.

It was so hot, without any breezes, that many of the crew set up cots on deck to sleep for the night.

April 26, 1994

The deck crew has started washing and painting the alleyways white. The whole ship's interior will be painted, white bulkheads and red decks. We have to be ready to present a ship in its best state when arriving in England.

The heat is tremendous, 94 degrees at noon with high humidity and only a slight breeze, while the temperature in the boiler room is up to 128 degrees. The boiler room must be constantly monitored by the Fireman water tenders (FWT) because of water, the fires and temperatures.

Everyone aboard seems to have a camcorder. I have been shooting every day at anything of interest. We note a bird about two feet high is standing on our bow preening his feathers while many of the crew stand by. It is completely unconcerned. Someone calls me and says take some pictures of the bird, I run forward and slam my head against the supports of the gun tub. You could hear it like a Chinese gong aboard the whole ship. Blood squirts over the deck and Ron hands me a cloth which is quickly saturated. Something for our doctor to do!

They take me to the hospital at the stern, get the doctor, and Greg acts as assistant. Pretty soon the audience is present and it is time to sew four stitches in my scalp. I never felt a thing, but never got the pictures of the bird, either.

April 27, 1994

We had the USNS Yukon, a naval oiler, signal a hello to us in the early morning. She was behind us and circled since she knew we were the Jeremiah O'Brien, the oldest ship still in ocean-operating condition, and she was the Yukon, the newest ship. Pictures were taken by her small zodiac of the two ships together, like mother and child.

April 28, 1994

The heat has abated somewhat, but we are still suffering from both heat and humidity, in the ocean without a sight of land. Everyone is soaked with perspiration and drinking their fill of the Gatorade and anything else available to make us feel human.

James Farras, the second cook, has a daily routine for lunches; soup and sandwich. Sometimes I look at the soup and ask what it's called. "Scrabble soup" is the response, meaning it consists of all the leftovers from the previous days, combined.

April 29, 1994

Finally there is a cool breeze, we enter some heavy rain showers and pass some of the Norwegian Cruise ships showing up only on radar. One ship calls us and says they have some seniors aboard, and with the coverage the Jeremiah is enjoying, they know what we are all about. They gradually and barely show up through the rain about a mile off starboard and we exchange whistle salutes as flash bulbs explode from their decks. Will they ever see those pictures through the fog? Our third mate Peter Knute Lyse speaks to the captain of the Cruise ship fluently in Norwegian.

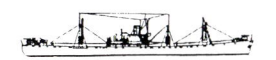

THE PANAMA CANAL

April 30, 1994

Arrival at Panama was 0918. We receive our pilot and slowly proceed toward the bridge of the Americas. We will tie up for the night at the Rodman Naval Base, hopefully to take on some oil for fuel. However, we soon find that the US Navy has put a hold on any fuel donations.

We are alongside a pier with a small nuclear sub on the other side, not a missile sub but one that goes to sea looking for drug traffic. Strange that the Navy is in this business, where is the Coast Guard?

We go ashore for a Coke, it has been a long time for that refreshment! We can use the local phones at military rates and many of us call home via AT&T direct to the US.

Today I make an important decision, I hope. The Jeremiah is in financial straits with lack of cash, and there are expenses that will have to be met in the future, like the planned expenditure of $500,000 at the shipyard before departure, which ended up costing close to $750,000. I speak to the Admiral about a plan to depart in Panama and go to New York and try to raise one million dollars. Certainly I would like to stay aboard but my time and efforts could produce more for the Jeremiah O'Brien if it's possible to accomplish what I plan. Can Eastern cities like Boston, New York, and others along the coast raise cash for the O'Brien while at the same time offering this traveling museum and National Heritage to a public viewing? Many well-known paintings and ancient artifacts are shown in the same manner.

I think it is a great idea and have confidence in my experience to pull it off. Next I approach the Captain, whom I should have approached first; he is in charge of the ship, and he is hesitant and is thinking of my giving up part of this trip of a lifetime. But I am persuasive and he agrees, as long as I feel so strongly about this possibility.

The O'Brien in the Canal.

May 1, 1994

The Captain, Admiral and First Officer appear wearing their whites; they are all very impressive in uniform.

Today we transit the canal. The Navy has set a plan for people assigned to the canal area. They are welcomed aboard the Jeremiah O'Brien on this Sunday to make the trip, see the 51-year old ship, and pass through the canal at no expense. Just bring along your own lunch, chair, and camera and the kids. Many of these people work or are stationed in Panama, and it is a way of offering a diversion from daily chores at no expense; a private boat tour of half the canal costs $65.00 per person. 75

visitors park at the Rodman Naval parking lot and come aboard at about 0800.

The canal is really a marvel of construction and planning. Ships are lined up to head north to the Caribbean. Kodak makes a fortune as we enter the canal and proceed through the Miraflores Locks. The ship is towed by the electric engines smoothly through the locks to Gutan Lake, where we proceed under our own power to the next set of locks. The air is clear, rain storms are on the horizon.

Ships traveling south to the Pacific pass us along the way, monsters from all countries of the world with their cargoes of oil, bulk products, autos, etc. A toot on their whistle shows their recognition of the 51-year old Jeremiah.

The last set of locks, the Gutan Locks, are congested and we anchor to await our turn to be brought down by three separate locks to the level of the Caribbean. Finally, we enter the locks and the process is duplicated. As we enter the waterway to the north we can see about fifteen ships waiting to make the their cost cutting trip to the Pacific. The total raising and lowering of the ship amounts to approximately 75 feet. The locks operate 24 hours a day.

As we get close to Cristobal we call for the tug, since we must tie up at a dock to receive clean fuel for the diesel generator, an out-of-pocket expense of $19,000. A steam pipe in the engine room develops a hole and the capable Chief Engineer and his assistants have the problem in hand in short order; no one is hurt.

The gangway becomes a problem since it is on the starboard side but the ship is laid against the dock on the port side. However, the organized deck department with the Bosun Ray just physically lift this whole gangway (weighing at least 1000 lbs.) over Hatch 5, and it is set for use. We don't realize how many visitors we took through the canal. Where have all these people been for the past twelve hours?!?

Navy buses are standing by for the long trek to the Rodman base at Panama City. I am packed and leave the ship to join in the free ride. It seems I made some friends while aboard, and I wish them all Godspeed upon the sea. I envy them the voyage ahead, but I know that what I have asked myself to do is more important for the Jeremiah O'Brien than serving food three times a day. We arrive in Rodman about 2300.

Also leaving the ship at Panama as planned is Steve Worthy, the First Assistant Engineer. He is so proud of the dedication of Cadet Dirk Warren that he requested a few days earlier that I make an award certificate to present to Dirk for his untiring efforts and time put in on any project requested. I must say it is something he could frame.

Steve is replaced by Tim Palange as First Assistant. Hans Miller the Third Assistant Engineer used his vacation time for this part of the voyage and is returning to his job in Oakland, CA. Replacements are the oiler Dennis Rodd and Chief Engineer Bill Maus, who has joined the ship in Panama as a Third Assistant Engineer. Robert Noisseux replaces one of the Third Assistant Engineers, there are always two Third Assistants on this cruise.

May 2, 1994

The ship departs Cristobal at 1700 hours and proceeds on its voyage; next stop, Portsmouth, England.

For me, this will be a day of planning to accomplish what I hope is practical and possible, and a day of travel. Tomorrow I will be putting all the plans in motion.

O'Brien deck 8-12 watch at Cristobal, Panama and their art on the dock done by Jean Yates. L to R: Sam Wood, Jim Conwell, Phil Sinnot, and Walter Jaffee.

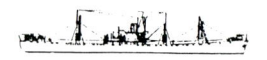

THE OTHER SHIPS

Unfortunately, the other 2 ships scheduled to join us in the "Last Convoy '94" could not make the voyage.

The SS John W. Brown

Costs to prepare for sea were tremendous, and the Shipyard where the Brown was originally built required prepayment, plus a guarantee payment for any additional unforeseen work.

When the Brown went into the dry dock, it was found that there was much more work required with the rivets on the bottom of the hull than had been anticipated. They determined they would require an additional $600,000 before they could be prepared for sea.

They did receive special permission to sail to New York City. When they departed, they had a boiler problem and had to anchor in NY Harbor for a short period.

The SS John W. Brown was able to make a voyage to Halifax, Boston, and Greenport in late August 1994.

The SS Lane Victory

They announced they could not make the voyage at their deadline, then they received a $250,000 gift and prepared for sea on May 1, 1994. They proceeded for six days when they developed an engine problem and had to pull into Acapulco. The delay was to be a few days but the problem was greater than anticipated, and the ship finally returned to San Pedro. They will escort the SS Jeremiah O'Brien as part of a welcoming party on September 23, 1994.

The TV State of Maine

The beautiful training vessel of the Maine Maritime Academy joined the Jeremiah O'Brien a few days before reaching Portsmouth, England with 250 officers and crew aboard. This ship took part in the "Parade of Ships" to Normandy.

59

CHAPTER IV

DAILY ROUTINE IN THE CARIBBEAN AND NORTH ATLANTIC

May 3, 1994

The weather is good with a slight chop to the seas, but the ship is averaging 10.4 knots at 65 r.p.m. The regular routine continues as work in restoring the beauty of the only unaltered Liberty ship is resumed.

May 4, 1994

The weather shows itself with a 10% roll, speed is reduced to 50 r.p.m. and 5.4 knots.

May 5, 1994

Half way to Mona Passage the weather has quieted somewhat. Peter Lyse, the third Mate, receives a call from the British ship Conchita

Jean with a cargo of New Zealand apples bound for Antwerp, Belgium. It has had a failure of its navigational gear and asks for a position. That's easy on the 51-year old Liberty, just read it off the Geographical Positioning System (GPS). Soon the other ship leaves us in its wake.

May 6, 1994

A quiet day, routine duties and normal speed. The ship can celebrate its birthday, the 51st anniversary of the keel laying of the Jeremiah O'Brien.

May 7, 1994

In sight of the Mona Passage with Puerto Rico on the starboard side. Only 3429 miles to go to Portsmouth. Now we face fourteen or more days without sight of land to merry old England.

May 8, 1994

Smooth sailing in calm seas. Jean Yates throws a bottle overboard with a message, where will it finally land?

May 9, 1994

Still calm sailing, the Bosun has the deck crew painting, making the ship more beautiful then it ever was. Seems there are many birthdays in May, each one is celebrated by the crew.

May 10, 1994

We received a message today that the Lane Victory developed engine problems off Acapulco and will be forced to return to San Pedro, Ca. A bearing valve overheated because the wrong oil was used in the wrong tank. We express our regrets. The convoy will now proceed with only the Jeremiah O'Brien, alone at sea.

May 11, 1994

Normal routine, normal duties, and calm seas add a calming effect to the crew. This is when you can enjoy the voyage and not be under pressure.

May 12, 1994

Today we rendezvous with the school ship TV State of Maine with 279 cadets plus crew aboard. She will be part of the 'Last Convoy' but will

TV State of Maine.

first stop in Ireland before arriving for D-Day ceremonies.

May 13, 1994

Another good day for sailing, putting us 274 miles closer to our destination. Normal routine is accomplishing our goal of being the best preserved ship for the Normandy fleet.

May 14, 1994

The sea is never boring; it's quiet and serene, a mystical quietness that is calming and thought-provoking. The day and evening linger on, you know it won't be long before you're ashore with your buddies, seeing new vistas, telling stories of past shore visits and enjoying the time off.
Now you're just 50 miles west of the Azores, and the heartbeat of the engines is in your ears, and you dream on.

May 15, 1994

James Wade our Anglican Minister, holds Protestant services at 1000 hours, which are well attended; later, he also acts as Priest for the Catholic services. At the request of Marine Superintendent Ernie Murdock, Carl Kreidler has a memorial service for the Armed Guard at this point of the cruise, where many Navy Armed Guard and Merchant Seamen gave their lives. We are now less than 1000 miles from Portsmouth, England.

May 16, 1994

The crew has been working together now for more than 30 days, four-hour watches for the deck crew and three hours for the engine department. Changing watches are considerate, at night lights are shaded, doors don't slam, and talking is hushed. New watches have their coffee while those relieved turn in for a good night's sleep. The daily routine is comfortable to all.

May 17, 1994

The weather becomes cool and foggy as we begin to enter the cooler waters near the coasts of France and England.

May 18, 1994

Today we sailed 248 miles at 10.7 knots. Odds and ends are being taken care of as we approach our destination.

May 19, 1994

Everything is ready aboard. Everyone has chipped in to bring one of the finest Liberty Ships ever built back to England to relive moments of her history. We have only 540 more miles to go.

May 20, 1994

We enter the English Channel two days ahead of schedule. Lands End is to the starboard, Brest, France to port. We are advised our dock is occupied and we will have to anchor before entering port.

May 21, 1994

The Jeremiah O'Brien anchors at the Man Of War anchorage in the Solent just off Portsmouth, England. The gallant ship and her crew have made it; the only surviving ship that took part in the Normandy invasion is here today to pay honor and commemorate the events of June 6, 1944.

The O'Brien will be able to dock on May 23. The crew is anxious to go ashore after 33 days.

The English people are just great, gracious would be a good description of their reception to all who brought the Jeremiah O'Brien this far and never lost their faith that the voyage could be completed. The volunteer crew and the Normandy '94 committee made it all happen, with the assistance of many, many people who may have had doubts but never gave up.

CHAPTER V

PORTSMOUTH

May 21, 1994

The SS Jeremiah O'Brien arrived at the Man of War anchorage in the Solent, a bay between the English coast and the Isle of Wight, ahead of schedule. She steamed 7552 miles in 33 days from San Francisco at an average speed of 10.2 knots. She went into the Historic South Railway Jetty in the Navy Yard and to the berth of the HSY Britannia, waiting for the D-Day events to take place.

The deal made with the Navy Yard was for a free berth, tugs, pilot, and admission. Although the ship depended on income from visitors, no Naval facility would allow charging of admission to any visiting ship. Having the ship in the Yard for Navy Days was a coup! We never would have had the visitors had we been at a commercial dock, besides paying for all the services required.

However, the British people were gems, and they catered to the crew with receptions and luncheons. The whole stay in Portsmouth was one party. The Navy Day celebrations went on for three days and drew thousands upon thousands of visitors. There were many fly-overs with World War II planes, a Lancaster bomber, Hurricanes, and Spitfires. Helicopters performed maneuvers that were astounding, such as perpendicular dives, flying backwards, and loops. The British aerobatic team added thrills, with up to ten flying jet fighters at a time in miraculous maneuvers. The crowds oohed and aahed at their flying skills.

A total of 26,000 visitors toured the Jeremiah O'Brien in Portsmouth, setting a new record. A blue line was painted on deck with arrows for visitors to follow. Following this line brought them to all the important positions on the ship from stem to stern, including the Bridge and Engine room, and before they left it took them to the Ship's Store. It was a well-organized route that alleviated traffic jams.

There is so much to see in Portsmouth with museums of all types spread across the city, Charles Dickens' birthplace, a D-Day museum, many ships in the shipyard, and large nautical museums in the shipyard itself. Visiting vessels include a Dutch and a German submarine, the USNS Normandy, a missile cruiser, and various antique ships. The most prominent museum ship was the HMS Victory, which is still commissioned by the British Navy. Admiral Lord Nelson was aboard during the Battle of Trafalger. He was subsequently wounded and died aboard ship.

A tour gave some idea of the life and times aboard the Victory, starting with seamen, a mere seven years old, who loaded powder into guns, pork that could be salted and stored for 10 years before being served, overheads that lowered as we went below to four-foot clearances, and hammocks within inches of each other. The ship is in excellent condition and quickly reminds a seaman of how lucky we are today.

Long lines were waiting at many ships; the O'Brien had the appreciated assistance of the British Sea Cadets, who offered their services for three days. Older visitors to the ship were appreciative and reminisced on what Liberty Ships meant to them and to England, bringing food and everyday basic supplies to the civilian population, but most of all American troops and supplies to end the terrible war.

Portsmouth was also celebrating the 800th year of the issuance of its charter; the combination of these events brought visitors from all over England.

In 1545, King Henry VIII watched his fleet engage the French in the Solent, a passage between Portsmouth and the Isle of Wight. His new warship, the Mary Rose, was launched with 700 aboard to fight the French. As the king looked on in horror, the ship rolled over for no apparent reason, and all aboard were lost.

About one third of the ship's port hull has been raised from its sunken bed after 450 years. It has been moved into a special temperature-controlled building with an elaborate watering system that sprays the wooden remains, keeping them wet as they would have been under the sea. In a few years, they expect to add resins to the sprays and eventually cover all the decaying wood in a plastic shield. Only the Americans and the British could take such a disaster and make it into a National Monument.

Dining in Portsmouth is a fine experience. Pubs are the choice for the lunch crowd, evenings are spent in any one of many excellent restaurants with four-star meals. One we enjoyed the most was the Sally Port Inn, with an intriguing 16th century decor. Inside, we found a very powerful painting that we all admired, entitled 'Women and Children First.' A large sailing vessel is sinking, its stern partly under water, while a seaman, his arms outstretched, is handing a crying child over the gunwale to a distressed mother in a lifeboat, her arms and facial features pleading and praying that she can receive her treasure. The seas are rough, making the transfer from ship to boat treacherous. It was a work we will all remember, as though it had been hanging in the Louvre.

June 1, 1994

A large flat bed truck approached the O'Brien. It contained a huge American flag, which was to be raised on the Jeremiah's boom between #4 and #5 hatches. However, the winds were very strong, and such a flag could never be raised. Mark Valentine, the driver, is responsible for this unit. He travels all over the world to raise this flag to bring pride to the United States.

A large space near the O'Brien, almost a city block in area, had a tent set up to provide beer and sandwiches, and seats to allow the visitors to rest their tired feet. At one end of this area, a large stage was erected for all types of bands. We were entertained by military and 1944 period music throughout the daylight hours, as long as the Navy yard was open.

We were informed by the US Coast Guard that only twelve guests would be allowed to make the voyage on the O'Brien to Normandy; meanwhile, the number aboard totaled more than 30. Eventually, the problem was resolved, and all aboard became known as business visitors.

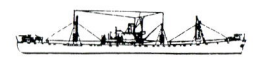

D-DAY MUSEUM

In Portsmouth, England, you will find one of the most amazing hand-embroidery achievements of this century. It commemorates the greatest invasion of all time, the ships, planes, and troops that landed on June 6, 1944 and helped bring about the downfall of the Nazi regime that had conquered Europe.

The idea was five years in the making and displays, in 34 panels, each measuring nine feet in length and three feet in height, the story of the D-Day invasion of Europe with some introductory panels showing the preparations for resisting the Germans and an ending panel of the liberation of the French. Each panel is dedicated to this period of the war and depicts in many sequences on each panel the battles and figures who were important during this particular time.

The hand embroideries were created by the "The Royal School of Needlework." Twenty embroiderers and five apprentices worked with

The commanders meet, February 1944.

linens, silks, and cords, stitching and appliqueing in many original colors to match the art provided for the Normandy invasion.

The collection, completed in 1973, is shown in a special building which overlooks the Solent, a bay where the invasion fleet had gathered before heading for the Normandy beaches. For a small fee you are admitted to the exhibition and supplied with a phone that describes each panel in detail. The work is beautiful, the faces of Eisenhower, Montgomery, Churchill, soldiers and civilians, etc., are works of art, the

The armada sails, 6/6/44; the Jeremiah O'Brien shows right center.

scenes are highly accurate with the finest detail. You can appreciate the time and effort employed in designing and drawing the panels, transferring them to the linens, cutting and sewing all the appliques. and hand-stitching everything together.

Should you ever be lucky enough to visit southern England, this is a treasure you would not wish to miss. The story in embroidery is similar to another in France, known as the Bayeux Tapestry, which shows an earlier period of time (although it is called a tapestry, it is also hand-embroidered).

The seaborne assault begins, 6/6/44.

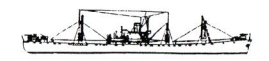

SOUTHAMPTON

June 1, 1994

The ship was moved to Southampton in readiness for the Solent anchorage. The Admiral requested my presence on the ship for the 50th D-Day commemoration. Of course, I was with my wife, so we cancelled our Rouen Hotel and Brittany Ferry reservations and changed our return to the USA from a Paris flight to a London flight.

The ship was active with Presidential Secret Service officers, and the FBI checked everything, even conducting an inspection of the hull by divers. The exact movements of the President when he arrives on board were thoroughly scrutinized. No part of the ship was exempt from study.

The Jeremiah O'Brien docked just north of where the Queen Elizabeth II would end its voyage from New York. The passengers included 500 veterans, the Kings Point Band, and a full passenger list, and

Secret Service checking the ship and planning the President's every move.

security was extremely tight. It was amazing to see this vessel docked as a textbook maneuver, with winds at 5-7. Three tugs turned the ship around and let the winds bring her parallel to the dock.

Unfortunately, because of their schedule, the 60 members of the Kings Point band could neither perform for nor visit the 51-year old Liberty, docked within a few hundred feet of the QE II.

Kings Pointers aboard the Jeremiah O'Brien, Portsmouth, England.

June 2, 1994

Thursday evening a reception was hosted on board TV State of Maine, and attended by O'Brien and Guam crews. We were lucky to have "docents," a number of British and Dutch Merchant Marine veterans who offered their

Graduates: Lane Kirkland (Pres. AFL-CIO), Retired Admiral Albert Harberger ('55 Maritime Administrator), Admiral Tom Patterson, and Captain George Jahn.

invaluable assistance.

June 3, 1994

A British World War II show and fair was taking place at the dock of the QE II. Crowds gathered for the music of the British marching bands, the fair, and the O'Brien. The crew was also invited to join the crew of the SS Shieldhall for lunch. The Shieldhall is another all-volunteer project. Her captain, Alan Swift, is an avid O'Brien supporter.

CHAPTER VI

IN THE SOLENT

June 4, 1994

The weather was rainy and overcast. The Port of Southampton, Associated British Ports, held a commemorative service on the pier. Large crowds stood in the rain as each of the five ships left quayside to the sounds of their National Anthems.

At 1200 hours, we single up then slide slowly out of the dock to the music of two British bands playing marching songs. They end with "The Star Spangled Banner." Film crews from the Japanese ASAHI TV and French TF1 were on board to film the event. All was still on the pier as Paul Dunnellon of the port stepped forward and said, "Thank you for 1944." There wasn't a dry eye in the crowd.

We proceed to the anchorage in the Solent; the winds are very strong. The Solent on June 4-5, 1944 was so packed with ships that, from the shore, you would think you could walk across the area, stepping from ship to ship. Today many ships could be seen, including the TV State of Maine, the Black Prince, the USNS Guam, the Vistafjord, and some

Cruise ships. We see the new US Aircraft Carrier George Washington close by at anchor. She was unable to dock in Portsmouth or Southampton because of the water depths. Later the QEII also joined us at anchor.

We are informed that President Clinton will come aboard the Jeremiah O'Brien on the 5th.

Our new aircraft carrier USNS George Washington.

Admiral Tom Patterson had written a letter to the President four weeks earlier requesting his visit; we feel it is a great honor, not only for us but also for the Merchant Marine. Such a visit will bring great press since no president has ever reviewed a Merchant Ship in history. Also, just think of the honor we receive as the first Merchant Ship to be reviewed by the Queen of England, who will be aboard her yacht HNY Britania.

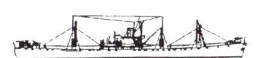

THE PRESIDENT'S VISIT

June 5, 1994

The winds are again strong. Today we will be reviewed by the Queen of England from her ship, the Britania, then we will be visited by the President of the United States. Private boats begin to build up in quantity as the day grows older. Every vessel you can imagine is sailing today. Some are 50 years old, some are foreign, one, the Starseeker, passes with a hand-painted banner stating "Thanks for our Freedom." A one-man kayak passes, a four-masted bark, an ancient steam side wheel vessel, the P.S. Waverly, modern pleasure boats; soon the water is churned into a white froth as the Queen's ship moves closer.

The crew will be stationed in two rows along the starboard side of the forward deck to greet the President. The "business" visitors and wives are on the after deck and will also greet the President. Both groups are told that no lunch will be served this day. This news is greeted with a loud groan.

Aboard ship, the crew practices our salute of "Hip Hip Hooray" and wave of the hat for the Queen's yacht. The active crew all have the same color golf shirts embroidered on the left breast with the Jeremiah O'Brien and caps embroidered in the same manner. As the Britannia approaches, we do our salute. An estimated 20,000 private boats turn the sea to foam.

The Royal Navy provided a barge for the President's boat to land. It is bobbing impatiently in the restless sea, which is too rough for a small boat to safely discharge guests. The harbor tug standing by pulls the ship perpendicular to the wind, forming an eddy and a smooth sea. Our gangway is secured.

The first boat to arrive is a small ferry with 40 or more newspaper and TV reporters to cover the occasion. They are given instructions by the Secret Service protecting the President as to where they can position themselves and how they are to cover this news event.

An NBC reporter was interviewing Ed Smith and began asking controversial questions about the President's veteran status. I walked away; it was not the time for such opinions. A few moments later, I was tapped on the shoulder and asked my name and address; something must have stuck in my head, because I ended my response with "Whitman country" (in reference to Christie Whitman, Governor of New Jersey). I think the statement was just what he was looking for, so he started with the veteran thing again, and he asked how I felt about a President who might have ducked being inducted into the Army. I gave him my opinion, which didn't satisfy him. He turned off the camera and gave me an idea of what he'd like to hear, then started the camera again and told me to put it in my own words. Well, I repeated my original statement: "My son received his draft number for the Vietnam war, and I had no idea what he would have done, since he was anti-war like everyone else at the time. It was up to him, he was twenty years old and it was his decision, not mine." The interview ended abruptly; however, it did air on NBC Evening News that day in Miami and New York, and maybe many more cities.

Soon we could see, in the distance, a scene from right out of a

The Presidential flag, held by Nat Taylor and Bill Duncan before the President's arrival.

80

James Bond movie, as four or five identical boats approached us with another four or five pontoon boats carrying scuba divers. Which boat was the President on? They all looked alike.

They tied up to the barge, and the President and First Lady came aboard. The Presidential Flag was raised by Nathan Taylor, our Kings Point Deck Cadet. The entourage was escorted to the Officers' mess, where Hillary immediately filled a cup of coffee for her husband. The President was presented with a Jeremiah O'Brien sweater and cap, the First Lady with a cap and a Limited Edition Commemorative Enamel Box, hand painted for the Royal Collection. We discovered that she is also a collector of this type of box. At the same time the new Merchant Marine Flag was raised on the ship for the first time.

The President, introduced by Admiral Tom Patterson, greets Otto Sommerauer and Jim Miller.

When President Clinton came on the forward deck he was very Presidential, standing straight while flashing the Clinton smile. He was personally introduced to each crew member by name by Admiral Tom

81

Patterson and shook hands with each one while a White House photographer took pictures of each greeting.

Following a few paces behind him, Hillary was also greeting each member individually. When she got to me, I said the same thing to her that I did to the President, "It is an honor and a privilege to have you aboard," but then I quickly added, "...and I am an original crew member of this ship from 1944." She stepped back, looked me over and said, "You must have been twelve years old!" Needless to say, she made my day.

The President, introduced by Admiral Tom Patterson, greets the author.

A short welcome was given to the President as he shook hands on the after deck. After only 21 minutes the Presidential party departed.

That evening the ship pulled anchor to start the voyage to Ponte du Hoc, France, across the English Channel.

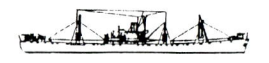

D-DAY NORMANDY

June 6, 1994: D-Day

At 0400 hours, we heard a lot of noise against the forward starboard hull as twelve veterans were transferring a boat to visit the USNS George Washington. I didn't know anything about this visit to the GW but heard the commotion against Hold #2, since that was where we

82

were bunked on this ship with a shortage of sleeping areas with 80 persons aboard.

The visit was another moment of pride for the Merchant Marine. The whole US Cabinet were aboard sitting in the first row, and the twelve Merchant Mariners, including Admiral Tom Patterson, Captain George Jahn, Admiral Albert J. Harberger, and AFL-CIO President Lane Kirkland, were in row two and chatted with the Cabinet members while waiting for the ceremonies to begin.

The President once again greeted the Merchant Marine Veterans, and he requested that Admiral Tom Patterson join in the wreath presentation services. It was a solemn occasion of reflection commemorating the 50th year of the greatest armada ever assembled in history.

In his speech, the President mentioned the shipyard workers who knelt on the deck of the Liberty Ship they were building to pray for those at the beaches on June 6, 1944.

It was a quiet day, spent wondering how the soldiers felt scaling those 100-foot high cliffs directly in the faces of the strongest German defenses on the French shore. The feelings were in the hearts of all, but words were not spoken. You could see the contemplation in everyone's demeanor. It was extremely quiet aboard. For Captain George Jahn, the only one aboard who was actually there 50 years ago, it had a great meaning.

There was no way any of us aboard could go ashore. There was a dedication on board to commemorate the loss of Navy Armed Guard and Merchant Seamens' lives during the invasion and those buried ashore at Arromanche, France. Father Wade read the Bible service, and Captain Jahn and Admiral Patterson, along with Carl Kreidler, dedicated the wreath to the sea. Admiral Patterson was asked by a friend to place a knife his son had not taken with him to the invasion into the sea at Pointe du Hoc, in remembrance of his death at this point. The father claims that, had his son had a knife with him, he could have cut his shrapnel-riddled life jacket loose and would not have died.

There was nothing to do the rest of that day, so the Captain ordered steam and the anchors were heaved as we left for the next port of call, Chatham. It seemed we were the only ship leaving the area, and as we passed the various French and American vessels at anchor, we dipped our flag to each vessel, which was supposed to respond in the same manner. Funny, none did.

The O'Brien steamed along the French coast, passing the US Cemetary at Colleville su Mer. That was the resting place of fourteen Merchant Mariners who lost their lives at Normandy. By early evening, we had to anchor off Margate Roads since the tides would not let us enter the Thames Estuary.

Admiral Tom Patterson was Master of Ceremonies of a special award program of Normandy remembrances held in hold #2. An invocation was made by Father Wade about our crews, past and present. "Memories of Normandy 1944" was delivered by Captain George Jahn,

Master of the Liberty Ship SS William Matson in 1944 at Normandy and the Liberty Ship SS Jeremiah O'Brien in 1994.

The award ceremony included the presentation to the SS Jeremiah O'Brien of an Operation and Engagement Star for participation in Bombardment of the Coast of France June 8-25, 1944, Reference Department of the Navy OP-23-1-bfc, (A) PERS ltr dated 27 Feb., 1945. The presentation of the Star was conducted by Carl Kriedler, United States Armed Guard, and Coleman Schneider, Deck Cadet SS Jeremiah O'Brien July 1943 to March 1944. This award service ribbon plaque has been added to the ship's name plate and to the service ribbons displayed on the top deck, both port and starboard.

All hands then joined in the singing of the Merchant Mariners' Hymn:

> Heave ho, my lads, heave ho,
> It's a long, long way to go.
> It's a long, long pull
> With the hatches full,

Braving the winds, braving the seas, braving the treacherous foe.

> Heave ho, my lads, heave ho,
> Let the seas roll high or low.
> We can cross any ocean, sail any river,
> Give us the goods and we'll deliver.

Damn the submarines, we're the men of the Merchant Marine!

A second song, "Eternal Father," was sung, followed by the Lord's Prayer.

The following morning, we left for Chatham, passing a sunken Liberty Ship, the SS Richard Montgomery, only its topmost masts visible above water, and still loaded with ammunition which has lain there for more than 50 years.

D-DAY 1944

Canadian corvette escorting convoy.

Pearl Harbor, 1941: the beginning.

Typical North Atlantic weather, 1943.

Convoy in the North Atlantic.

D-DAY 1944

Queen Mary at D-Day.

Capt. De Smedt and Frank Pelligrino at D-Day.

Unloading at Normandy.

Many Liberty Ships were purposely junked to form a "gooseberry" to protect landings and the unloading of lighter craft from the forces of weather, wind, and waves.

D-DAY 1944

Landing, D-Day.

Defense for chemical attacks.

Nat Taylor, 1994 cadet
Coke Schneider, 1944 cadet
Marci Hooper, business manager
Dirk Warren, 1994 cadet

Original cadets, 1944.

D-DAY 1944

WORLD WAR II POSTERS

CHAPTER VII

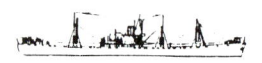

THE CADET

I always liked the sea, and, at fifteen years old, I became a member of the Sea Scout Ship Ranger in North Bergen NJ. They had an old barge on the Hudson River where meetings were held on Friday evenings. This was in 1939, when things were heating up in Europe and war was near.

Our officers were great teachers; I am astounded today that I can still tie some of the knots and splice a line. Some of the members had their own small sailboats and we all learned to sail. We also had some lifeboats we salvaged from old ferry boats. The crew grew steadily and reached 75 members.

We studied, we practiced, we had competitive regattas. Every day after school, we spent time at "the Barge," and weekends as well. We painted it, built walkways, built a head, fixed up a galley, and painted its name on the sides.

We needed a boat for more than four people, so we decided to look for one of the used boats advertised for sale on the Jersey shore. In four or five cars, twenty of us drove to various boat yards, looking for something we could afford that was still in good condition. Nothing we could afford existed. On the way home, we stopped at a lookout point for this photo, then returned to West New York, where most of us lived. The radio was announcing Pearl Harbor; the date was December 7, 1941.

The Sea Scouts were an active group, and six of us were seniors in high school. For Boy Scout Week, we decided to wear our scout uniforms to school. On Tuesday, February 9, 1942, there must have been fifteen of us in our Sea Scout uniforms, which looked very much like those the enlisted Navy man would wear.

December 7, 1941. Top row, 3rd from left: Eric Fisher. Bottom left: Coke Schneider, the author.

The Memorial High School at West New York, NJ, overlooked the skyscrapers and passenger terminals in Manhattan, and we always saw the main ships come and go, like the Bremen, Europa, Ide de France, Queen Mary, Mauritania, Rex, Conte di Savoia, Georgic, Aquitania; in other words, the leading passenger ships, carrying traffic to and from Europe in first-class comfort, sadly replaced by those lovely airplanes of today.

School was out at 3 PM, and we noticed the large plume of smoke rising from the French liner Normandy, the fastest and most beautiful of the large passenger ships. Six of us decided to cross the river to get a better view. It was five cents for the bus to the ferry, and ten cents to cross. The dock was within two blocks of the ferry exit.

We walked through the Police and Navy lines; I guess we looked like them in our uniforms. Each of us assisted the New York Fire Department on board. Finally, two hours later, we were told to leave the ship, as she began to list to port. It was time to go anyway, as some of us had part-time jobs. She keeled over and sank that evening.

After graduation, I worked for some months on a New York Railroad Tug, now atop a hill at the Cape Cod Canal.

The idea for our own boat was settled when a fellow who had built his own 40-footer and was tied to the Roselle, a sunken barge on which we kept our boats, said he would assist in the construction. We raised money with a dance and chance books. Without plans, we proceeded to build a 36' lap strake all copper-riveted boat with 1" and 1 1/2" planking. We started in late February and launched the finished hull in April. Everyone worked constantly, after school and on holidays and weekends.

More and more members were being drafted or enlisting, and the boat, now tied to the dock, would have to wait for our return. As high school graduation approached, we wondered what service we would join for war duty. My friend Eric Fischer, who was also involved in the Normandy fire and whose family was active in the shipping industry, applied at and was appointed to the USMMA at Kings Point.

Looking over my options, and with three brothers in the services already, I also chose the USMMA. My first ship was the Liberty Ship SS Jeremiah O'Brien as deck cadet, with James D'Andrea as engine cadet, on its maiden voyage. We were reassigned to Kings Point after the third voyage, since we had nine months' time in. Her next voyage was to D-Day 1944.

After graduation, I was assigned as third mate to the Liberty Ship SS Henry S. Foot for one voyage, then the Lykes Bros. ship MV Cape Nun, which returned to New York in late 1945.

How was the war experience on the SS Jeremiah O'Brien (and the others)? Simply wonderful; we never saw a torpedo-firing or a sinking, and we were never bombed. We did have horrendous storms in the North Atlantic, with 30- and 40-foot waves and strong winds which proved the stability of the ship and the crew's handling of her. Many times we did lose the Plimsol makes under the water when loading. We depended wholeheartedly on the US Navy and Air Force, who were our protection. The story would fit the book by Studs Turkel, the "Good War" for an eighteen-year old visiting half the world and having the chance to do it again 50 years later.

To receive my Pilot's license, I gained time on the Army Engineers dredge Goethals in New York Harbor. The exam was not too difficult, but what was difficult was trying to secure a job with one of the Pilot Associations with a first-class unlimited tonnage license and no experience and no relatives in the field.

For a while, I went back to the Erie Railroad and shaped up for jobs on tugs, which made no sense when one job I had for a week and shaped up daily for was taken away by an actual drunk who slurred his words, saying, "Ish got schenority" ("I got seniority"). Thus ended my sea career.

But, I was still active in the USNR and did sail a summer exercise on the DD McDougall, on which President Roosevelt and Mr. Churchill met in 1940 to write the Atlantic Charter. My sea experience on the Liberty Ships saved us from cancelling that voyage to Montreal because of the bad weather.

A recall for Korea was cancelled, since I had a number of employees in a one-man operation. I was discharged in 1957 from the USNR as lieutenant sergeant.

USMMA KINGS POINT, 1943

Barracks were the first housing.

1943 Cadet Coke Schneider.

Center: Delano Hall.

Bottom: Barry and Jones Halls.

95

AT SEA 1943 - SS JEREMIAH O'BRIEN

Above: Entering Firth of Clyde through protective nets.

Dec. 24, 1943: Coke Schneider, Rubert Milby, 3rd ass't. engineer Watson.

Time for refreshments: Coleman Schneider, 3rd ass Watson, James D'Andrea.

96

TV Emory Rice

TV Gresham

TV William Webb

KINGS 1944 POINT

1944 - "Sound Off" KP newspaper. Left to right: Coke Schneider, Business Manager, Charles Blanck, William Westin, Joseph Hassinger, Jr. Seated: Edward G. Stack, editor.

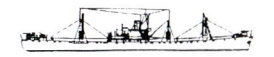

RAISING FUNDS

The cost of operating the ship from Europe and back is unbelievable. Fuel alone is costly, running upwards of $500,000. Thousands of barrels were required. Maintenance of the ship, putting her in dry-dock to clean her hull, repairing underwater valves, welds, etc., painting the hull, updating her 1943 safety standards for the Coast Guard to 1994 standards; costs for all these ran over $750,000. All these items do not include the food for 56 crew for six months, and adding fresh supplies in foreign ports.

Spare parts for a ship 51 years old cost ten times what they did in 1943.

When entering ports, you incur costs for the Pilots, Tugs, and dockage. Add to that the security required, usually provided by independent shore personnel.

There is insurance on everything in sight.

Most important are the extras you never consider until something goes wrong.

The Jeremiah O'Brien was lucky, since a CAT Diesel was loaned to the ship, along with a satellite system and radar.

The all-volunteer crew could never have covered these costs by themselves, and sponsors are always needed for larger sums. Income is derived from admissions and sales from the ship's store, special short sightseeing voyages, and hirings for special events. It isn't easy, and the ship is usually in debt.

If you would like to help in a small way, please fill out the form on the next page, and you will receive a plaque in appreciation.

SS JEREMIAH O'BRIEN

P.O. Box 625
Tenafly, NJ 07670

201-313-0022
800-526-0411

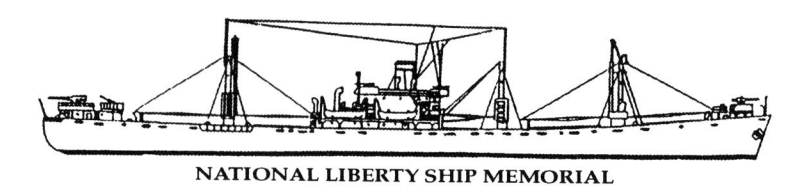

NATIONAL LIBERTY SHIP MEMORIAL

Help us to buy the fuel to bring back our national monument from England, where it participated in the 50th anniversary of Normandy. Then we can arrange visits to ports on the East Coast.

IN RECOGNITION OF YOUR GENEROSITY...

You will receive a Plaque or Certificate of Sponsorship inscribed with your name.

- ❑ $100.00 Silver walnut plaque 7" x 9"
- ❑ $200.00 Brass walnut plaque 7" x 9"
- ❑ $500.00 Silver walnut plaque 10" x 12"
- ❑ $1000.00 Brass walnut plaque 10" x 12"
- ❑ $_____ Donation

❑ $25.00 Unframed certificate
❑ $50.00 Walnut framed certificate

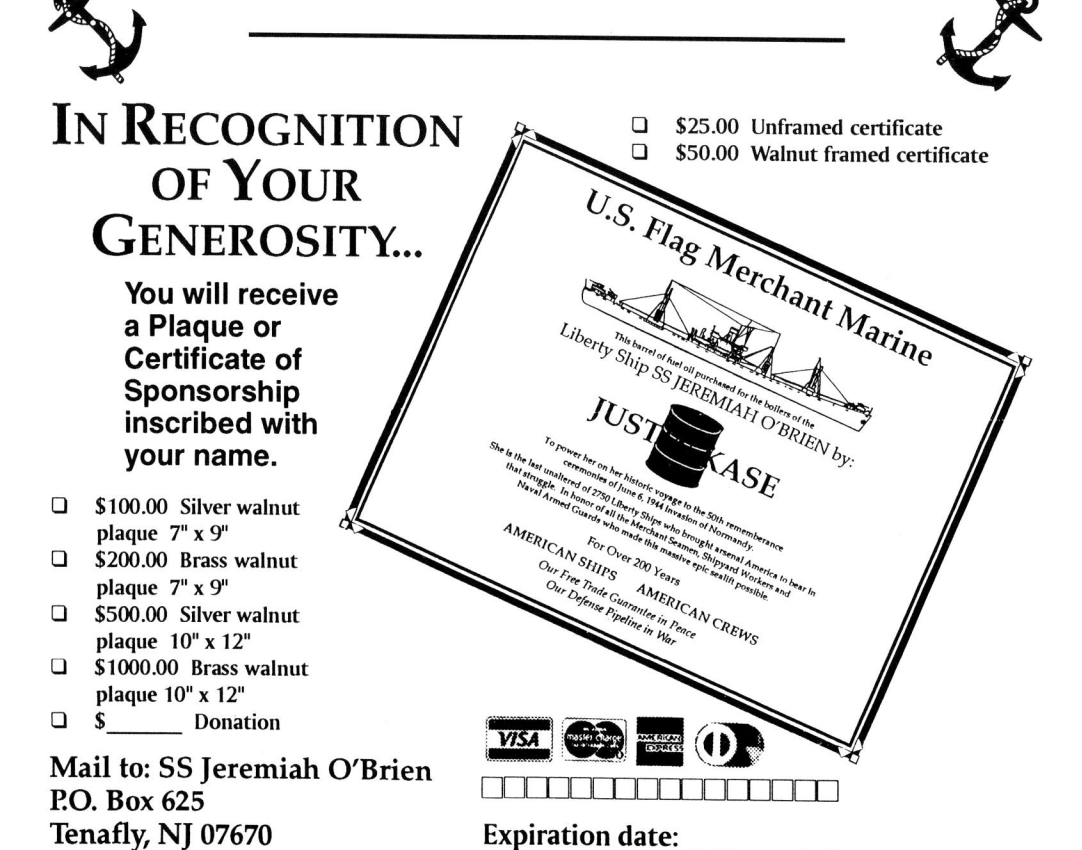

U.S. Flag Merchant Marine

This barrel of fuel oil purchased for the boilers of the Liberty Ship SS JEREMIAH O'BRIEN by:

JUST ___ KASE

To power her on her historic voyage to the 50th remembrance ceremonies of June 6, 1944 Invasion of Normandy. She is the last unaltered of 2750 Liberty Ships who brought arsenal America to bear in that struggle. In honor of all the Merchant Seamen, Shipyard Workers and Naval Armed Guards who made this massive epic sealift possible.

For Over 200 Years
AMERICAN SHIPS   AMERICAN CREWS
Our Free Trade Guarantee in Peace
Our Defense Pipeline in War

Mail to: SS Jeremiah O'Brien
P.O. Box 625
Tenafly, NJ 07670

VISA master charge AMERICAN EXPRESS [Discover]

Expiration date: _____

The beginning of the National Liberty Ship Memorial SS Jeremiah O'Brien 1980

SS JEREMIAH O'BRIEN

Saving the Last Unaltered Liberty Ship

by

William D. Sawyer

and the

National Liberty Ship Memorial

San Francisco — 1980

101

SS JEREMIAH O'BRIEN 1980

The O'Brien in the Bethlehem Yard, S.F., 1980.

The cadet room, untouched in 36 years.

Captain McMichael.

Harry Morgan, Chief Engineer.

50th ANNIVERSARY

50th anniversary celebration at the Presidium, S.F. L to R: Mrs. Jaffee, Yvonne Schneider, Admiral Tom Patterson, Coke Schneider, Capt. Walter Jaffee, Marci Hooper, business manager NLSM.

Promotion and identification are the most important products that can be used to raise funds. Never miss a chance for a photo session, seminar, or interview.

Make the name of your trophy known to anyone and everyone.

The "other" Liberty Ship,
SS John W. Brown

*The
volunteers of
Project Liberty Ship
extend their heartfelt thanks
for your help in the reactivation
of the S.S. JOHN W. BROWN. We
share with you our pride in bringing
this fine old ship back to life as a living,
steaming memorial to those who built, sailed and
defended the WW II Liberty Fleet.*

EPILOGUE

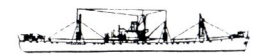

The voyage did not end after D-Day. We left the Normandy coast about 1300 hours and proceeded to Chatham. We were informed the entrance to the Thames Estuary could not be entered for another twenty-four hours so we were forced to anchor off Margate Roads, England.

Before dinner was served, beer was offered to those who could appreciate a busy day winding down, and a small party ensued. 1944 music was playing on a Sony, and a few of the men danced the Lindy with some of the girls present. We found a wooden pole and had Nate Taylor, our KP cadet, do the Limbo. When the chimes announced dinner, the party ended.

The next day, we proceeded to the locks of the Chatham Maritime, where we found dozens of people waiting for the ship to be tied up so they could come aboard. When the ship was secured, a local TV camera crew on shore started asking, where is Coke Schneider? The rush was to make the evening news. I gave my thirtieth interview since coming aboard in Frisco.

Channel pilot Captain Brian Lukenhurst and Marci Hooper, business manager.

My wife and I departed the ship and stayed in a hotel room ashore. It must have been the fourth time I said goodbye to the ship, but I ended up

107

for some reason or another going down to the ship every day and saying goodbye once again.

I decided to rent a Cessna 150, and took Michael Emory, the self-proclaimed photographer, along to get some pictures from the air. Strange, the lowest we were allowed to fly in England was 1400 feet, whereas in the US it's 500 feet. We were able to make one low pass over populated areas without giving the owner a heart attack. Only one thing was wrong; I forgot my camera, and I still haven't seen the pictures Michael took!

After four days, the ship moved to London for five days, then Cherburg for another five days, Rouen for seven, and Le Harve for five. This completed the European phase of the voyage, and the ship then went to sea to cross the Atlantic to Portland, Maine. The southern route was taken because of storms in the North Atlantic. She arrived in Portland on August 6 after a quiet voyage with calm seas, and she stayed there for six days. I visited the ship in Portland, which proved an interesting and profitable stop for the O'Brien.

At this point, I knew they wanted to make a dash for Baltimore; everyone was getting antsy to return to their home port. I asked if we could plot a course to bring the ship south through the Cape Cod Canal, and the Long Island Sound, to Kings Point. I suggested no stops and full speed where possible. At Kings Point, the ship could anchor overnight, then through Hells Gate, the East River, the Upper and Lower New York Bays, and along the New Jersey Coast. At the south end of New Jersey, they could proceed up the Delaware Bay to the Delaware Canal and thence to Baltimore. It was complicated, and Captain Carl Otterberg suggested I lay out the plot and contact the four pilots requested and make sure there would be no costs.

For the 51-year old ship everyone was willing to help; pilots, tugs, and dockage were given freely. They chose this route, and I think the main reason was that we could anchor overnight at Kings Point. The Admiral had been a deputy superintendent nine years earlier, and the other graduates on the ship would be pleased, while the crew could learn something about the U.S. Merchant Marine Academy.

At the same time, the only other Liberty Ship, the SS John W. Brown, planned a cruise to Halifax and would be entering the canal from the west entrance on Sunday at 1200 hours. The O'Brien was to enter the east entrance on Monday about 1500 hours. They made radio contact in the Atlantic and were able to make a visual sighting, the only two seagoing Liberty Ships remaining of the 2751 built blowing their steam

Photo by Provo Wallis, Canadian Coast Guard.

whistles in greeting to each other. The passing through the Cape Cod Canal drew hundreds of visitors, and they were also greeted by whistle blowing for the length of the canal. It was dark as they entered the Long Island Sound and arrived at Kings Point about 0900.

The Coast Guard had the O'Brien anchor near Stepping Stone Light which was quite a distance from the Academy. I was informed by Superintendent Admiral Tom Mattason of the arrival of the O'Brien and drove from N.J. to Great Neck as the Admiral and Captain Robert Safarik were getting ready to leave for the ship. Three AMMV members from the Dennis Roland Chapter also took a ride on the Academy skiff, piloted by Lt. Cmdr. Eric Wallischeck, to the O'Brien.

The officers got into their whites and came ashore about 1300. Ceremonies for those 142 cadets lost at sea during World War II were made before the plaque bearing their names. A second ceremony was held in the Chapel for the 6000 seamen lost at sea during the same war; visitors and crew members attended these ceremonies. Short speeches were made by Admirals Mattason and Patterson and Captain George Jahn. The crew was then invited to a party at Wiley Hall at 1900 hours, where they all had a good time.

Admiral Tom Patterson greeting the public and explaining the role of Liberty Ships in WWII.

The O'Brien departed at 0600 while the tide was slack at Hells Gate, then proceeded

Congresswoman Helen Bentley and Maritime Deputy Commissioner Joan Yim supporting the Jeremiah O'Brien.

110

south down the East River alongside the skyscrapers of Manhattan. They steamed down the New Jersey Coast through the Delaware Bay and the Delaware Bay Canal to Baltimore. I owed them some embroidered Caps and Golf shirts and drove there to deliver. Once again, some goodbyes, but this was the last till San Francisco.

After four days they left Baltimore for Mayport, Florida, ending the visits on the East Coast. On August 28, the O'Brien departed for the Panama Canal. They then stopped at San Diego because they were way ahead of schedule, before entering San Francisco on September 23, ending the voyage of a lifetime.

San Francisco had a ticker-tape parade in the afternoon and a great welcoming party on Pier 27 in the evening with all the sponsors of the voyage and crew present.

WELCOME HOME!

APPENDIX A

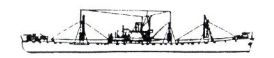

LOG SS JEREMIAH O'BRIEN

DEPARTURE: Southwest Marine Yard, San Francisco, CA
Monday, April 18, 1994 1200 hours

DAILY	DISTD	POSITION	TEMP	WIND	SEA	BAR.	LOCATION
To noon:							
4/19	259	34.05 N 119.30 W	54	NxNW	4	1071.1	Off Pt. Conception, CA
4/20	273	31.01 N 116.52 W	50	NxNW	3	1015.3	Off Cabo Colonatt, Mexico
4/21	289	26.52 N 114.39 W	62	NW	1	1015.0	Off Bahia de Ballenas, Mex.
4/22	269	23.36 N 111.05 W	66	NWxW	1	1013.4	Off Cabo San Lucas, Mexico
4/23	282	20.41 N 107.03 W	76	W	1	1012.5	Off Cabo Comientos, Mexico
4/24	261	18.05 N 103.12 W	82	W	3	1012.0	Off Pt. Peehilinguilo, Mexico
4/25	277	16.02 N 98.53 W	86	Airs		1010.1	Off Punta Maldonado, Mex.
4/26	287	13.49 N 94.28 W	84	W	1	1010.1	Off Sacapulco, Mexico
4/27	284	11.43 N 90.12 W	82	Calm		1019.8	Off Punta Guiones, San Sal.
4/28	262	9.45 N 86.15 W	79	Airs		1010.1	Off Cabo Valos, Costa Rica
4/29	261	7.35 N 82.27 W	81	Airs		1012.3	Off Isla Montuosa, Panama
4/30 - 5/1				S	2	1010.9	Balboa Harbor
5/2							Cristobel Harbor
5/3	157	11.01 N 77.51 W	85	NE	4	1009.8	At sea, Caribbean
5/4	137	12.36 N 76.11 W	83	ExNE	6	1009.5	East of P.R., Mona Passage
5/5	172	14.16 N 73.48 W	82	NExE	5	1011.8	At sea, North Atlantic
5/6	189	16.10 N 71.12 W	80	E	3	1013.9	
5/7	219	18.15 N 68.09 W	84	E	2	1015.8	
5/8	254	21.12 N 65.05 W	77	NE	5	1017.1	
5/9	259	24.19 N 61.52 W	78	SExE	3	1019.1	
5/10	256	27.22 N 58.36 W	75	ExSE	4	1022.9	
5/11	261	30.20 N 54.57 W	74	ExSE	3	1024.0	
5/12	263	33.09 N 51.04 W	71	SxSE	3	1024.8	
5/13	284	36.00 N 46.44 W	70	S	3	1024.7	
5/14	262	38.37 N 42.21 W	81	SW	3	1023.2	
5/15	275	41.04 N 37.16 W	63	SE	3	1021.8	
5/16	276	43.24 N 31.55 W	62	S	3	1020.0	
5/17	256	45.16 N 26.33 W	55	SE	5	1011.6	
5/18	257	46.55 N 20.57 W	60	SExE	2	1001.5	
5/19	248	48.12 N 15.10 W	57	NxNE	4	997.2	

5/20	238	49.17 N	9.27 W	55	ExNE	4	999.2	
5/21	241	50.05 N	3.10 W	52	NE	2	998.1	
5/22	93			54	SxSW	4	1008.2	Anchored in Solent
5/23 - 5/30								At Portsmouth, England
6/1 - 6/3								Shift to Southampton, Eng.
6/4				53	ExSE	3	1005.5	Anchored in Solent
6/5				60	W	3	1020.9	Anchored in Solent
6/6				63	SW	3	1018.0	Anchored off Pointe du Hoc
6/7								Harbor of Chatham, England

APPENDIX B

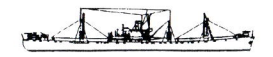

VOYAGES OF THE SS JEREMIAH O'BRIEN

After approval of sea trials, the SS Jeremiah O' Brien sailed from Portland, Maine to Boston, Massachusetts. The first voyage of the O'Brien departed Boston, MA on July 20, 1943. She proceeded alone to Halifax, NS, Canada, to join a convoy to England. The first stop was at Loch Ewe, Scotland, then Methil, Firth of Forth, Scotland and finally she discharged her cargo at London, England. The return was via, Methil, Firth of Forth, and then Lock Ewe. There she became part of a convoy to New York. Two days out, she developed problems with her boiler tubes, left the convoy, and steamed independently to Gourock, Firth of Clyde, Scotland for repairs. In a few days, she returned to a westbound convoy for New York, NY arriving on September 11, 1943.

The second voyage departed New York, NY after shifting to Bayonne, NJ to load ammunition on September 14, 1943. She sailed in a convoy directly to Liverpool, England to discharge her cargo. The return was again in convoy directly to New York, NY arriving November 3, 1943.

The third voyage departed on November 19, 1943, the day after Thanksgiving, from Staten Island, NY in convoy directly for Lock Ewe, Methil, Firth of Forth, to Immingham, England to discharge cargo on December 24, 1943. The return in convoy was to Lock Ewe, Scotland directly to St. John, New Brunswick, Canada. The third voyage continued, since such voyages can only terminate when the ship returns to a United States port.

After taking on cargo the third voyage continued from St. John to Halifax, Nova Scotia, Canada independently. On this trip, she was hit by a storm with high seas and heavy winds which brought huge quantities of water aboard. With sea water at 28 degrees, ice quickly built up on the decks. We were concerned for the ship's safety as the ice grew thicker, as can be seen on the photos. Within half an hour, every ice chopper on the ship was broken, but luckily we made it to Halifax, Nova Scotia, Canada without further problems.

The Captain, Oscar Southerland, left the ship here, and Captain A. A. De Smedt became the new Master on Jan 20, 1944. Frank Pellegrino, the Second Mate, required hospital care and was replaced by the Third Mate, Oliver Morgan, who was replaced by Russel J. Smith as the new Third Mate before we departed in convoy. The convoy sailed to Oban, Scotland, then Leith, Scotland to discharge its cargo. The return in convoy was to Lock Ewe, Scotland then directly to New York on March 24, 1944.

At this time the cadet/Midshipman (the author) had accumulated nine months' sea time on the SS Jeremiah O'Brien. During WWII, sea time was to be six months for a cadet/midshipman or until the ship reached an American port; then he had to return to complete the course at USMMA at Kings Point, NY.

The fourth voyage began on March 25, 1944, with loading in Brooklyn, NY. The voyage in convoy sailed to Gourock-the-Clyde, Scotland then to Southampton, England. The O'Brien then made eleven crossings of the English Channel from various English ports and one from Belfast in Northern Ireland to Utah and Omaha beaches, each time bringing troops and supplies to the Normandy beaches. The return voyage began at Cherbourg, France to Mumbles Point, Swansea, England, Milford Haven, England then to New York, NY arriving on October 12, 1944.

The Jeremiah O'Brien made three more voyages for a total of two and a half years of service, which ended her career on January 17, 1946.

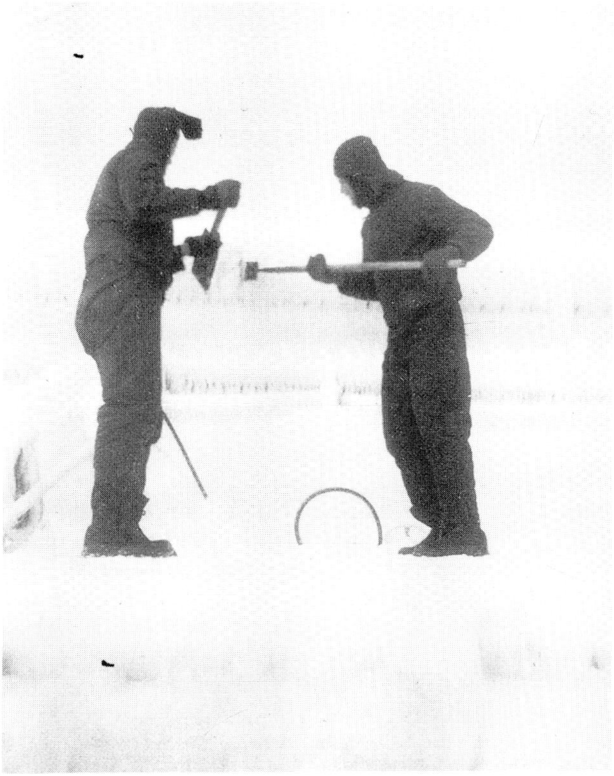

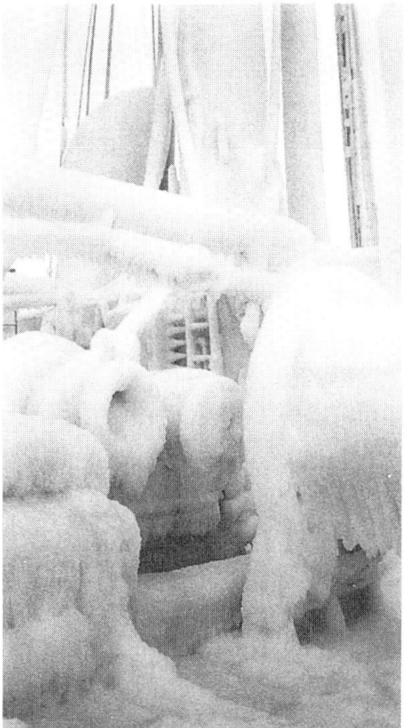

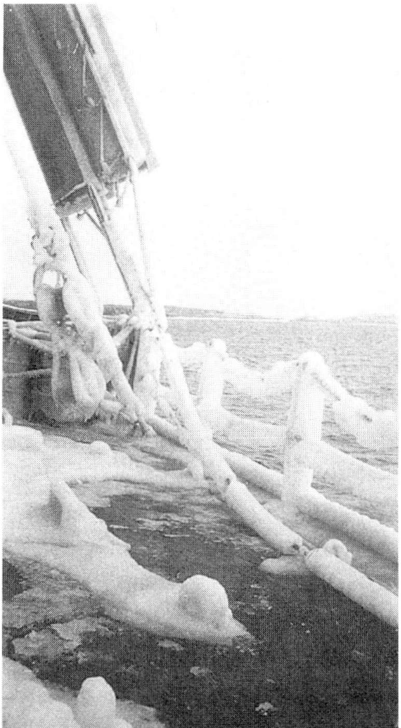

THE MUSEUM SHIPS

The Liberty Ships SS Jeremiah O'Brien (San Francisco, California) and SS John W. Brown (Baltimore, Maryland) and the Victory Ship SS Lane Victory (San Pedro, California) are the only existing World War II Merchant Ships operated by all volunteer crews and wholly self-sufficient. They depend on donations from individuals and sponsors to maintain themselves.

The US Merchant Marine sustained the second largest losses of life in World War II and carried 95% of the cargo required for the Army, Navy, and Marines who so gallantly fought to erase tyranny and bring peace to Europe and Asia in 1945.

Let us not forget our Merchant Marine in peace as well as in war; let us make it strong, keep it viable. Next time, we may not have the time and determination to build a whole fleet of working ships.

THE SHIP'S STORE

Ron Robson in charge

Purchasing agent for the successful ship's store on the Jeremiah O'Brien

Ruth Robson and Dotty Duncan.

Art Taber, manager.

Ed von der Porten, Michael Smith, and Saryl von der Porten.

REPLACEMENT CREW MEMBERS

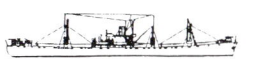

INDEX

A

Allendorfer, Captain Harry	7, 8
American Bureau of Shipping	40-44
Armed Guard	39, 84

B

Bentley, Helen	10
Boylston, John	10
Blake, Bob	7
HSY Britania	66
Bush, President George	10

C

Carter, President Jimmy	8
Clinton, First Lady Hillary	81, 82
Clinton, President Bill	77-82
Coast Guard	41-45, 70
Conchita Jean	60
Crew	12-39
Crowley, Tom	7-9

D

D-Day Museum	70, 87
del Becq, Andre	10

G

George Washington	13, 77, 82
Gibbs and Cox	3

J

Jahn, Captain George	8, 13, 84
John W. Brown	10, 16, 20, 33, 42, 66
Johnson, Clint	10

K

Kings Point	3

L

Lane Victory	10, 42, 44
Last Convoy	10

M

Machias, Maine	1
MARAD	5, 6, 7
Margaretta	1
Marriner, Gayne	7
Merchant Marine Act	2
Mikulski, Barbara	10
Moor, Captain	1
Morgan, Harry	7
Murdock, Captain Ernest	7, 10

N

National Liberty Ship Day	8
National Liberty Ship Memorial	7
National Park Service	7
National Trust for Historical Preservation	8
NBC	80
Normandy	91, 92

P

Patterson, Admiral Tom	6, 11, 14
Pearl Harbor	14
Portsmouth Naval Base	5

Q

Queen Elizabeth II	72, 74, 75
Queen Elizabeth II	77

R

Reserve fleets	5, 6, 10, 14
Robert E. Peary	3

S

Sea Scout Ship Ranger	90
State of Maine	59, 62
Suison Bay	6

U

U-boats	2
"Ugly duckling"	3

V

Vernick, Joseph	10

W

World War II	2